AFTER GENOCIDE

—there is hope

AFTER GENOCIDE
—there is hope

Mary Weeks Millard

Terra Nova Publications

Published in Great Britain by
Terra Nova Publications International Ltd.
Orders and enquiries: PO Box 2400 Bradford on Avon BA15 2YN
Registered Office (not for trade): 21 St.Thomas Street, Bristol BS1 6JS

Cover design by Roger Judd

ISBN 978 1 901949 54 4

Printed in Great Britain by
Creative Print and Design Group
Harmondsworth

Contents

ACKNOWLEDGEMENTS

I dedicate the book to my husband, The Reverend Malcolm Millard, thanking him for all his encouragement and patience through the months of research and writing.

My special thanks goes to The Reverend Stephen Gahigi, for sharing his story, and to The Reverend Jean Paul Ruzindana for his help with translation, The Most Reverend Emmanuel Kolini, Archbishop of Rwanda, for writing the Foreword to the book, and to The Reverend Nathan Amooti for making it all possible.

Foreword

by Emmanuel Kolini
Archbishop of Rwanda

As his Bishop, it gives me great pleasure to be able to commend this book about Stephen Gahigi. He has been a priest in my diocese since 1998. I had the privilege of ordaining him as priest in that year.

For almost a decade I have grown to know him well. He is remarkably gifted as a man, and naturally intelligent. Also, despite the huge difficulties in his life he has remained steadfast to the Lord and his calling in Christ.

As you will read, he lost 100 cows at the time of the genocide, as well as having one of his children shot in his arms, but showed no fear as he sought safety with his child. He left like so many others did. But he came back.

Since those difficult days he has developed a diverse ministry that covers a range of interests, from reconciliation to pastoral care, to work in prisons and the military. For instance, he ministers to military officers with love and integrity.

But he also works with survivors, as well as ex-prisoners and their families, which he seeks to bring together for sharing, reconciliation and dialogue. He seeks to unite brothers and sisters on both sides of the ethnic divide. Not unlike Christ would seek to do. Gahigi is a pastor to everybody, beyond his own painful past.

In a friendly and honest way he does not fear challenging and questioning people. Which means he is highly respected, with a large parish and a successful congregation. He is a faithful pastor, but especially to those who have been devastated by the genocide.

I am proud to commend him to you as the reader. His story is a most remarkable one, and well deserving of being told to a much wider audience than this book will allow.

May he and you continue to be blessed in Christ.

Emmanuel Kolini
Bishop of Kigali
Archbishop of Rwanda

March 2007

Preface

The plane was coming in to land and I could see the panorama of hills and valleys, small red roads winding up the hillsides, then a greater concentration of houses as we approached Kigali. I stepped off the plane at Kanombe airport and walked over to the arrivals building, and at once the smell of the damp, warm African soil greeted me. For those who have not had the privilege of visiting Africa, it is hard for me to explain! The smell thrilled my being and I knew I was back in what has become my second home, the small country of Rwanda.

I have been visiting Rwanda regularly since 2001, under the auspices of Signpost International, a Christian organisation which cares for families and children at risk, and have grown to love this 'land of a thousand hills' as it is affectionately called. I have also grown to love and admire the people, who have suffered such horrors through genocide, but who are now working so hard to rebuild their lives and country. Most of my work has been teaching health and related topics to the women and older orphans, something I love to do.

This time my visit was to be different. I had been asked if I would be willing to come and write the story of an Episcopalian minister, Pastor Stephen Gahigi. I was delighted to comply, because I have known Stephen since my very first visit to Rwanda, and been greatly impressed by his humility and his spirituality. I had heard something of his remarkable story and was eager to learn more and to share it with a wider audience.

This book is the result of that visit. Even in researching and writing it I have been challenged and changed. My prayer is that it will be a blessing to all who read it.

Mary Weeks Millard
Kigali
January 2007

SONNET TO RWANDA

O Africa, cradled within your heart
Lies a place which has wound itself round mine,
Rwanda, a jewel you stand apart,
'Land of a thousand hills', with views sublime.

Yet, you shelter within your valleys there
Your weeping children, burdened with their pain;
Dark hillsides absorbing the secrets, where
Slaughter and murder have left bloody stain.

In serenity the banana grows
Silent witness to your fertility,
While in the byre the new born calf now lows;
Life has regained some normality.

So brother, in forgiveness, let there be peace,
May love return and hostility cease.

Mary Weeks Millard, 2007

Chapter One

Growing Up

This story begins in 1963, in what was reputed to be the most deprived area of the republic of Rwanda, the region of Bugesera. This district was renowned as a bad place in which to live, a place where the tsetse fly thrived and caused the disease of sleeping sickness. Much of the area is swamp, but most of the remainder is dry, arid and difficult to cultivate. This was the district where many of the ethnic group of Tutsi had been forced to live. It had been a definite policy of the Hutu dominated government in the 1950s to relocate these people to this area, hoping that they would become sick and die. They wanted to make life as difficult as possible for them, and planned to exterminate them in the course of time.

In this area of Bugesera, near the main market town of Nyamata, a baby boy, Sitefono Gahigi (Stephen), was born to Kalemera Augustine and Nyiradende Merecaine. He was the third child in the family, having an elder sister and brother. In many ways it was not a good time to be born, because there was so much unrest in the country and the Hutu controlled government of the day were implementing this orchestrated campaign to gradually exterminate the Tutsi people. The families in Bugesera felt insecure, with friends and relatives disappearing without trace from time to time. People woke each day knowing the fear within them that this day could be their last day alive on this earth. Stephen's family knew they were under threat, that they might be the next family to be targeted for extermination. It was because of this threat that soon after Stephen was born his father went into exile in Burundi. He knew his life was in danger. He had survived one or two attacks on his life already, and these had left him with bullet wounds in his chest, so it was just a question of time before his attackers were successful in killing him. He felt his only course of action was to flee into exile. Rwanda is a small, landlocked country, bordered by Burundi, Congo, Tanzania and Uganda, but the Burundi border is the nearest exit point to Bugesera. The people of Burundi also had the same ethnic groupings and spoke a language almost identical to Kinyarwandan, the language of Rwanda. At one time, the two countries had been one, so these factors made it the country of choice for exile for Stephen's father. So, one day, he packed up a few belongings and set out to walk to the border. It was not an easy choice, but he felt it was the best thing he could do for himself and his family at that time.

Of course, this meant that Stephen's mother was now left alone with three small children for whom to care, and also a very large herd of cattle to supervise. She, too, lived in fear for her life. Fear was like a black shadow cast over the family, and a mantle of hopelessness fell on their lives, so much so that even the small children were aware of it. All Stephen's early years were shrouded in this fear. The family struggled through from day to day as best they were able. They tried to put a smile on their faces and carry on with the routine of daily living. What else could anyone do?

More than three years passed before Stephen's father felt it was safe for him to return home again. In exile his life had been safe, but the bullet wounds he had sustained before he fled from Rwanda had become infected and he returned a sick and broken man. It had been a very difficult time for him, and he was so glad to return to the family. When he arrived home, although the family were pleased to see him and gave him a wonderful welcome, he was to find that things were far from well. The home he had been so proud of had been looted and his very valuable herd of Ankole cattle stolen. His wife had been defenceless against the looters, so most of the furniture and household goods had been taken, as well as many of the precious cows. Wealth in Rwanda for the Tutsis was measured (and still is, to some extent) in the number of cows owned, and so losing them was akin to losing all your money and the inheritance from your parents which you cherish and pass on to the next generation.

So it was that little Stephen grew up living in this time of great insecurity. He acknowledges freely that it had an impact on his emotional life from the very start. Even when his father had returned home, when perhaps it might have been thought that things would improve, the shroud of fear which encompassed him persisted. Father was such a broken man – living without hope and always in fear of death – that he was unable to give his children the security and sense of safety which is every child's birthright. When asked for a word to describe how he felt about his early years, Stephen's reply was, "hopelessness". The early years of childhood which should be happy and carefree had been blighted. He and his siblings were children growing up under a cloud of ethnic hate. They felt their people were doomed, and death would eventually come to them in one way or another. They somehow sensed they were living under an unspoken death sentence, even though they were still very young children.

Politically, the country was in turmoil and dominated by the growing strength of increasingly radical Hutu political parties. In late 1963 it is estimated that up to 10,000 Tutsis were killed in sprees of ethnic hatred. Violence was the 'norm' of daily life in many places in this beautiful land. The 'thousand hills' were absorbing horrible secrets, which seemed to be unnoticed or disregarded by the outside world.

I am only recording the story of one person in one family, but almost everyone I meet in Rwanda has a story to tell of fear, hate, loss and tragedy. This is a country with a legacy of sadness and pain, of a build-up of ethnic mistrust which emerged from time to time like the horrific eruptions of a volcano, destroying everything in its path. It is, however, the story of a person who has found an answer to combat the distrust which echoes around those thousand hills. It is also an answer to the fear and mistrust which many of us can find in the hidden recesses of our own hearts, although we live in such different circumstances.

Stephen's father was a very hard working man, and after his return he sought to make life better for his family. In spite of his poor health, he set to work to establish a banana plantation on their land. When the bananas were in fruit, he cut them and took them to sell in the market at Nyamata. Bananas form part of the staple diet in Rwanda. There are cooking varieties, called *matoke*, small and larger sweet bananas, and bananas which are grown mostly for fermenting into the local beer. If a person has enough land to grow bananas, they supply a good source of food for the family and provide a regular income.

Gradually, Stephen's father was able to replenish his herd of cows, as his cashflow increased. The Tutsi people are traditionally cattle herdsmen, and their cows are prized possessions for a family. Stephen and his brother would be schooled from a young age in how to care for the cattle, for they would become their inheritance.

His own family grew in size, too, as three more girls and two more boys were born to him and his wife. It was still a difficult time for the Tutsi people, but there was more peace and stability in the home than during the early years of Stephen's life. It seemed as if prosperity was returning and politically there was less harassment.

The family were animists, believing in and worshipping 'nature spirits'. They made frequent visits to the witch doctors to try to buy peace for their troubled hearts. When they went to visit these shrines it was expensive, because they had to take along animals or food, to pay for the sacrifices, which their family could ill afford. However, they were convinced that if they did not do this their family would be cursed and even greater calamity might befall them. All the time, they were longing to know some sort of inner peace in their home and family life. They made the required sacrifices, but it still eluded them.

The Tutsi people were known as *inyenzi* (cockroaches). It was a byword of hate that was hurled at them wherever they went. It was a way of degrading and dehumanising these people who had once been the ruling class in the land and had boasted kings and proud warriors. The Tutsi monarchy had lasted almost 800 years, and had wielded absolute power as the ruling class.

Many Tutsi people have a noble bearing, being very tall and slender. Their very height has been seen as intimidating by their neighbours, and the memory and oral tradition of story-telling about the history of the kings and how they treated those under them has rankled with the Hutu people for a long time.

There was no school in the village where Stephen lived, so when he was around eight years of age his parents decided it was time for him to go to school. It was not compulsory for a child to attend, and many boys stayed home as goatherds or cowherds. Schools were fee paying, and a child's parents needed to provide uniform:

a blue dress for girls and khaki shorts and jacket for boys. The pens and exercise books also had to be provided. All in all it was an expensive business to send children to school, especially as most families had as many children as possible.

The nearest primary school was in the market town of Nyamata, where Stephen's older sister was now living. His parents decided to send him to live with her. This sister was already married, and she and her husband were very happy for her young brother to live with them. For Stephen, he was glad to be able to go to school, and he loved the lessons. The school itself was a very large government primary, offering only very basic teaching in Kinyarwandan and French.

There was a problem in the school because politics was also invading the classrooms. As the school was in Bugesera there were about equal numbers of Hutu and Tutsi children attending, even though, overall in Rwanda, the Tutsis represented only twenty per cent of the population.

For many generations the two ethnic groups had intermarried, and probably there were very few pure blooded Tutsis, but a child took its ethnic background from the father, and this was what was recorded on the identity card.

The teachers tormented the Tutsi children, calling them out and making them identify themselves as 'cockroaches'. Since Stephen was very tall for his age, and this being a distinguishing feature of a Tutsi child, he was subject to ridicule and discrimination even from the other children. The bullying brought back all the stories his father had told him after he had returned from exile, and fear and hopelessness fell, once again, like a blanket over his spirit, stealing even from the joy of now being able to attend school. All the terrible memories of babyhood returned. The sense of living under the threat of death was ever present. Nevertheless he persevered, studying and learning as much as he could in his classes.

The government requirement was that everybody carry an identity card, which stated the person's ethnic group. There were very random ways of determining this, by crude measurements of facial features. So Stephen now carried an identity card stating his ethnic group – that he was Tutsi – and it was almost like carrying a death warrant around in his pocket.

In previous generations, belonging to the Hutu or Tutsi group of people was more about class than ethnic division. The Hutu people were traditionally cultivators of the land; and the Tutsi, cattle keepers. A Hutu man could become a Tutsi by acquiring many cattle. The Belgian rulers first introduced the ethnic identity cards and arbitrary measurements that determined which group a person might belong in. They wanted to change the balance of power, and had begun to indoctrinate the Hutu people, making them believe that the Tutsi were their enemies and had treated them like slaves through the centuries. They had begun a divide and rule policy which tragically ended in genocide.

After independence, the Hutu dominated ruling party continued to enforce the regulations as a means of preparing for their policy of extermination of the Tutsi people.

During these tense years people sometimes mysteriously disappeared. Always in Stephen's mind as he grew up was the thought: would it happen to him? Would it happen to his family?

Stephen progressed through the six primary classes, and enjoyed studying. He would have liked to have continued and enrolled into the secondary school, but he was a Tutsi, and places in secondary schools were given to Hutu youngsters. Very few Tutsi children were allowed to continue with their education. If a Tutsi child was fortunate enough to be given a place in senior school, it was the school that chose the child, and the place would be offered to a child who had not achieved well in primary school, rather than to a bright child. The policy of the day was to educate the young Hutu so that they would get the senior jobs in trade, commerce and politics. They were destined to be the 'ruling class' from now on, and the Tutsi people very much the 'underdogs'.

Chapter Two

The Gathering Storm

The roots of the ethnic division began in the early days of colonialism. After the first world war, the colonies of Germany were divided up and given to other ruling powers. Rwanda, in 1885 as part of Ruanda – Urundi, had been assigned to Germany as part of German East Africa, but in 1919 was handed over to Belgium to administer. The Belgian colonisers built up the infrastructure and gave a local government administration structure, founded schools, churches and hospitals, for the next forty years until independence was granted.

The Germans, and then the Belgians after them, retained the ethnic power structure and class system, keeping the Tutsi king and his aristocracy in place. Gradually, the Belgians undermined the authority of the *mwami* and his chiefs, which caused unrest and hostility and destabilised the country. In 1931 the *mwami* Musinga was forced by the Belgian government to abdicate in favour of his son. His son, *mwami* Mutara Rudahigwa, was more of a puppet king and certainly had a more Westernised outlook on life. He converted to Catholicism, and remained as the figurehead until his death in July 1959.

The three ethnic groupings within the country had some distinct physical differences, although intermarriage had blurred these to some extent. The people groups were called: BaHutu (the 'Ba' denotes plurality – one person is called a Hutu), BaTutsi, and BaTwa. The BaHutu were agriculturists, the BaTutsi were cattle keepers and the BaTwa were of pygmy origin, and traditionally potters. The groups were a class system, too. The Tutsis were the ruling class, although a minority group, the Hutu were a much larger group and they became increasingly restless, feeling that they were second class citizens. The Twa were looked down upon by everybody, and counted almost as non persons. They are a small minority people group related to the pygmies of the Congo, and on the whole were not involved in the conflict of 1994.

It was in the 1930s that the Belgians began to make crude measurements of the facial features of the population, and to grade them into the three ethnic groupings, issuing identity cards. Everyone had to carry their identity card with them at all times. This system of classification continued right up until the genocide.

In the 1950s, more and more educated Hutus began to demand equal rights for their people. They wanted the Hutu people to be recognised as the majority group and the ruling group in the country. At this time the Tutsis were still advantaged in education and therefore occupied most of the top jobs.

Throughout Africa the cry was for independence

from foreign rule. Rwanda was no different, and in 1956 the king (the *mwami*) campaigned for freedom from Belgium and for an independent Rwanda. He wanted independence for his country, keeping the Tutsis still as the ruling class, but by now the Hutu leaders were calling for political reform, and had formed their own political parties, backed by the Catholic Church, which was very powerful. Belgium then backed the Hutu leaders, whereas before they had always backed the Tutsis and favoured them.

After the death of the *mwami* in July, and again in the following November, some violence broke out. It was the first anti-Tutsi uprising and resulted in around three hundred deaths, and a lot of homes being looted and burned. It was a grim shadow of things to come, and many educated Tutsi people fled into exile because they recognised there was little hope for their families to progress under the then present political climate. People who had been relocated to areas such as Bugesera were not allowed to move to another part of Rwanda, and if they went into exile they were forbidden to return and vote or serve in the armed forces. Refugee camps were formed in Congo, Burundi and Uganda to house the fleeing Tutsis.

Elections were called for and took place in 1960, in which one of the Hutu parties, the Parmehutu party, gained control. These elections were not recognised as valid by the United Nations, so were re-held in 1961 under their scrutiny. The Parmehutu party again won the election with Gregoire Kayibanda as leader.

Later that year in Butare, the university city of Rwanda, five thousand homes of Tutsi were torched, twenty two thousand people displaced and one hundred and fifty murdered.

By now, one hundred and thirty five thousand Tutsis had left Rwanda, and among them was a little boy of three, Paul Kagame, who was destined to help turn things around in the fullness of time.

In 1962, Rwanda finally was granted independence from Belgium, and Gregoire Kayibanda became the President. Rwanda might have lost the Belgian rulers, but had been left with a legacy of growing ethnic hatred and violence. The seeds of genocide had already begun to be planted.

Some of the refugees began insurgent raids over the borders into Rwanda. These brought swift reprisals to the Tutsi community, and in the latter half of 1963 there was another massacre of approximately ten thousand people. It was a pattern of violence that was to be repeated all over the country in the following years, culminating in the 1994 atrocities.

In 1965 President Kayibanda had been successfully re-elected, and the Parmehutu party had continued in power, although under the new name of MDR (Mouvement Démocratique Républicain). The new minister of defence was Juvenile Habyarimana. Under Kayibanda's rule, hostility towards the Tutsi people continued to such an extent that even some of the moderate Hutu people became alarmed. Corruption was rife, and ethnic cleansing was encouraged. One of the deliberate policies was now not just to intimidate but to expel all the Tutsi children from schools and colleges. It was this issue that led the minister of defence, Major General Juvenal Habyarimana, to stage a military *coup d'état* in 1973.

He became the new leader of the country, establishing a single party MRND (Mouvement Révolutionaire et National pour le Développement). Moderate Hutus and the Tutsis who still held positions of responsibility were unhappy at the move away from democracy, but Habyarimana was a puppet leader, ruled by his wife Agathe and her powerful family, and they decreed a one party state.

Things seemed to improve for a short time, but it was an uneasy peace. The evil of racial hatred had taken hold in much of the country, but especially in the Bugesera district, and the random killings continued. Even school children were targeted, not just being expelled from school, but even being taken and murdered.

Stories were reaching Bugesera of mass killings in another area, the Gitarama district. There were tales of houses being burnt down and houses looted. Fears were growing that the violence would spread to Bugesera, and the Tutsis lived under a dark cloud of apprehension. No one could trust his friends and neighbours any more, sometimes not even their own family.

Stephen recalled his thoughts and his feelings around this time. He always had questions in his mind: "What have we done that this should happen to us? Is it our fault? Have we sinned? Are we a bad people?"

With the questions, to which there were no apparent answers, there was also a growing hatred of the Hutu people in his heart and mind. Every Hutu, even neighbours and previous friends, now became potential enemies. Now when he saw them he asked himself whether they would be the ones to come and destroy his home and family. Stephen lived in an atmosphere of growing suspicion and distrust. He was rapidly becoming a bitter and angry young man. He could see little hope for his future.

One day Stephen's father came up with a good idea. Knowing that his son really wanted to continue with his education and attend a secondary school, and that there was now no chance of this happening in Rwanda, he made plans to take him to Burundi. He could go to school there!

It seemed a wonderful answer to the problem, and would give the boy the chance he deserved. He was bright and intelligent and should have the opportunity to make a future for himself.

So, they made their plans and prepared for the journey to cross the border. His father would take him, and they could walk there in a day. Stephen's father still had friends and contacts there following his years of exile, so he contacted them and the arrangements were made. Stephen was excited at having the opportunity to continue with his schooling. The anticipation was growing within him as the days drew nearer for his departure.

Then, disaster happened. Just before they were due to leave Rwanda, his father was involved in a car accident and died from the injuries he sustained. It was terrible! Stephen had lost his beloved father, and now had no prospects for his life; all his hopes and plans had been dashed. He had been so excited about going to Burundi with his father. He had felt hope rising in his heart, even lifting off the blanket of despair that had beset him for so long, but now in one stroke of fate he had lost forever the father he loved and the hope of further education was destroyed too. Pain, trauma and hate were filling his heart and mind.

His mother tried to console him as best she could, even as she wrestled with her own grief. "Never mind, my son. You are strong and young and you will survive. Here you have land and property and cattle. You will be able to survive and make a life for yourself here in Bugesera."

Her words were not much comfort and did little to help Stephen at that moment in his life. What she said was indeed true, the family by now owned a large herd of cattle, and Stephen took over the work of caring for them.

The plantation his father had worked so hard to build up was now a successful business venture. Stephen took over the day to day management of the plantation and the farm, becoming quite a wealthy young man, but life was never the same for him. His heart was not in what he was doing. Living with constant fear of the future made him feel that such work was a hopeless pursuit. In his mind he reasoned that he might as well just get what fun he could out of life while he was still alive.

Having money in his pocket, as he prospered in his farming, did not do Stephen any favours. He soon found himself spending it on beer, cigarettes and a pipe, and also frequenting the houses of prostitutes.

"When you are young and have so much money to spend and very little education, it is easy for you to get into very bad ways," explained Stephen to me, "and I did just that, and in fact, by so doing, I increased my own inner pain. I tried to drown my sorrows by drinking, and was soon known in the area as a drunkard."

He stopped to show me quite a large scar, close to his right eye. "This is due to drinking," he said. "I fell over one day, blind drunk, and cut myself badly."

Stephen was finding out, like so many before and since, that these things did not ease his inner pain or give any satisfaction, they just blotted out the painful thoughts for a short while, and so made life a little more manageable in the short term. As soon as he was sober, all the fear, anger and frustration returned. So the days turned into weeks and years, and Stephen was known as the 'wild boy' about town.

The years passed by, and in 1985 he began to feel it was time he settled down and found a wife for himself. He talked it over with his friends, but they all realised that he had one big problem. He had no Christian faith! He was still practising witchcraft, faithfully obeying the instructions of the witch doctor, offering sacrifices in his house, even though it gave him no peace of mind. His friends all counselled him: "If you want to marry a girl, these days they will only look at a churchgoer, so you had better get baptised! All girls want a church wedding nowadays!"

This was true, the girls were much more interested in attending the church services than the young men, and they wanted men who went to church, expecting them to make better husbands.

Stephen went away and thought about this advice, and decided if that was what was needed, then he would go to a church to find a wife. Two of his younger sisters had recently started to attend the Anglican church at Maranyundo, a village on the main road near Nyamata, as had his elder brother, so he decided it must be a reasonably good church to attend. One Sunday he plucked up courage and went along, asking the minister on his first visit if he could be baptised. There was no change in his heart or his ways, he was just doing what he thought was necessary in order to obtain a good wife. He started to look around at all the single girls in the church, and he saw a girl whom he really liked and he thought very pretty. Her name was Francine, and she soon showed that she was interested in getting to know Stephen. They began to talk to each other, first through a 'go-between', as is the traditional Rwandese way. It was Francine who eventually suggested that they married, even though that was not the conventional way of proceeding! In order to keep his young lady happy and not lose her affection, he lied to her and assured her that he was a baptised Christian. After telling her that, Stephen needed to arrange for his baptism to take place as quickly as possible.

Naturally Francine was upset when she realised Stephen had deceived her, and he was not in fact a Christian at all. When the baptism took place, her comment was that part of her was very happy, and the other part very angry! "I just wish you had told me the truth!" was her rebuke to him. She had hated being deceived, but was so glad that he was now eligible for marriage. Her desire to marry him was greater than her anger at his lies. All was arranged and the baptism took place, but for Stephen it was just a means for an end.

Immediately after the ceremony, Stephen travelled to a village some distance away, where he thought nobody would recognise him, and drank himself senseless. He recalls how he struggled home and fell asleep in his shoes! His baptism had not changed his heart at all, it had only given him the piece of paper he needed in order to marry the girl he loved. He thought he had done all that was necessary to become a Christian.

Francine's parents, although strong church attenders, were not true believers and were liberal and easygoing in their attitudes. They knew that Stephen had a certain reputation for being a 'boy about town', but they were not opposed to the marriage. Francine had not had a conversion experience herself, and was happy enough that her fiancé was now baptised and attended the church, and she could have a church wedding. So the couple proceeded into the months of courtship and the preparations for the wedding day.

Chapter Three

A Curse is Broken

Stephen and Francine were married in Maranyundo Church in July 1989. Stephen was twenty-four years old and Francine was nineteen. This was the culmination of a Rwandese style courtship. First there had been the introduction wedding, where the two families met and agreed the terms of a bride price. The dowry was agreed at one cow, for by now cows were scarce. Stephen so wanted his bride that he took along six of his very best cows and allowed Francine's parents to choose the one they thought the finest. Then there had been a 'giving away' ceremony at the bride's home, where she was put into the care of Stephen and his family. From now on this was to be her family. Traditional conical baskets were filled with rice and sugar, etc., and given to the young couple, and the bride's family helped with the other things needed to set up home. Sadly, all the photographs of these ceremonies, as well as the conical baskets, were destroyed when their home was razed to the ground during the genocide.

Just before the wedding, things began to change in Stephen's life. He found himself attending the services at the church in Maranyundo whenever they were held. One day he was at a church conference and the minister was preaching about inner peace. He explained that many people claimed to have peace in their lives, but really had no peace. The message was speaking into Stephen's heart, and stirring him up. He felt very angry inside. The lifestyle he boasted about made him out to be 'Mr Big', a macho man, who loved to show off in front of others. He was still a heavy drinker, and worked as a very successful trader. He exploited his customers, cheating them and lining his own pocket all the time, and so continuing to grow rich. He also had a reputation to live up to — he was well known and admired by the young men in the district.

When he heard the message given by this preacher, he thought that if he repented and changed he would be sure to lose all his money. So he went home very angry and started to blame his sister and his friend who had taken him to the meeting. Why had they taken him there? Did they want him to become poor?

In his mind and heart he was arguing, and trying to forget what he had heard. He wanted peace, but did not want his life to change. This battle within him raged for some days, and then he returned to the conference again. This time, as he listened, there came a response from his heart. He could not fight with God any longer. From somewhere deep within him came tears, not just a sob or two but a huge river, a flood of tears. In Rwandese culture, tears are hidden, they are a source of shame, and especially a man does not cry! Yet in deep conviction of sin and repentance, Stephen wept and wept unashamedly before the Lord, and the tears brought a cleansing and relief which even now he finds hard to explain. Something very deep and very real had happened in his innermost being.

He went home and back to work and tried to find words with which to tell his family and friends what had happened inside him. They did not receive the news very well and told him not to get involved and definitely not to change his life. He was doing well for himself, and in spite of the political climate of Tutsi persecution, he was becoming a rich and prosperous man. They did not want him to change his ways. So now Stephen had a dilemma to face. Should he continue to speak out about this new experience that had so touched his life? His friends were fast becoming estranged, and soon would be enemies. What mattered most, his new found peace and faith or keeping his old friends?

The pressure he faced from these friends was so great that he ran away once again to a place where he would not be recognised and drowned his problem by drinking. After this drinking bout he was walking back, worse for wear, when he heard a voice speaking to him in his mind, "Hey, who do you think you are hiding from?"

He knew the voice was the voice of Jesus. It was very distinct and direct. He knew that Jesus was challenging him. He could not run away from himself, or others, or from God.

Stephen felt very weak and indecisive as a Christian, so he sought out some friends who were also Christians and who attended Maranyundo Church. He told them about what was happening, how he could not take the pressure of opposition, and that he had resorted to drink, and he asked them to pray for him. He needed prayer that he would be strong and not fall into temptation. He confessed how he had gone on another drinking binge. Publicly, before his new Christian friends, he repented. They joined together and prayed for Stephen, that he would know the Lord's help and strength to walk the Christian way. They committed themselves to support him by prayer, not just at that moment but day by day.

Their prayers were a comfort and a strength, and then Stephen was able to tell the Lord, "You are right! You win! I cannot run away or hide from people, and definitely not from you!"

There was another area of his life with which Stephen was having a struggle. He had to remain continent as he waited for his marriage to Francine, but strong sexual desires had been awoken in him from the time when he used to visit the prostitutes. Now he begged his friends once again to pray for him, so that he could be pure until his marriage, because he knew that he was unable to resist this temptation in his own strength.

On the days when he visited Francine, he always made sure he was sober, and so she was not aware of the depth of the problems with which he struggled, nor that her future husband was known as a drunkard. He desperately wanted to marry her, so he tried to be very careful when he was with her. Her parents most certainly would have heard about his drinking by this time, but made no move to end the engagement. He was still a fairly wealthy young man who would be a good provider for their daughter; they were willing to 'turn a blind eye' to this personable young man's failings.

Stephen sat quietly for a few minutes before he continued to tell me his story. He wanted to be completely honest and tell me what he was really like at this time of his life. He wanted no 'whitewash', although he was very ashamed of the life he had lived in his youth. He went on to relate to me: "One day, my own mother, even though she was a pagan and drinking was normal amongst men, talked to me about my excessive drinking and advised me to get a grip on myself and stop it. She would not have reproached me, but she could see the harm it was doing to my life," he explained.

In Rwandese culture, everyone has a great respect for their elders, especially their own parents. Stephen sadly told me, "I replied to her in a terrible way, abusing her verbally. I was such a bad boy. It was a very terrible insult to throw at my own mother."

He recalls that, after finding that Jesus could help him and his life began to change, he went back to his mother's home and begged her forgiveness. Even the thought that he had treated her in that way made him very sad. He was glad that she had forgiven him, and he had the opportunity to be a good son to her in the days that followed.

Those early days in his faith journey were full of

struggles for Stephen. Most of his family were still worshipping spirits and consulting the witch doctors. As the time for the wedding drew near, another family row broke out. It was traditional to seek the blessing of the witch doctor to determine if the marriage will be a success. Indeed, it was so important that not one but three witch doctors were called. They spent an entire day performing their incantations and 'prophecies'. The result was that they said to Stephen, "If you go ahead and marry this girl, you will die on that very same day. You must accept our predictions, or you will be doomed."

The power of such black magic must not be under-estimated, for Satan does use people who are given over to his work. Often such curses do happen, unless they are refused in the name of Jesus, who has forever conquered Satan and his forces.

Stephen was such a new Christian; when he heard the prophecies he felt very scared. He had seen the results of curses which men such as these had put on others. He went again to his close Christian friends and asked them to surround him with prayer. He had yet to experience that the Name of Jesus is greater than any other in the universe.

These witch doctors gave him some herbs to put into the new house where he would take his bride. If he did survive his wedding, then they promised that his wife would be barren unless he obeyed them. Then, as an afterthought, they added, "If your marriage becomes successful, then we will give up our witchcraft."

On the night before the wedding was due to take place,

the beginning of a miracle happened. Stephen's mother spent the whole night crying. She was overcome with fear because of the predictions of the witch doctors and because Stephen had refused their magic. What would happen to her son? Did he really have a stronger power within him, in his faith in Jesus? She began to think about the Christian message.

The wedding day dawned at last. As requested, Stephen's Christian friends came to the ceremony and they surrounded Stephen with prayer, asking that the power of God would keep him safe. They, too, understood the power of the curses that witch doctors cast, and, like Aaron and Hur in the Bible, they supported Stephen in prayer all through the ceremony. Francine, his beautiful bride, was waiting for him in the church, and they were married without incident. As for his family, they were not only sharing in a wonderful wedding, but they were seeing a miracle unfold before their very eyes. They were all expecting Stephen to collapse and die that very day! They were so utterly amazed when he walked out of the church alive.

Once again, when their predictions failed to materialise, the witch doctors' response was, "Just wait, your wife will be sterile, she will bear you no children."

Stephen's response was to speak about this latest curse with his friends, and they continued to pray with him and for him. The power of prayer was being demonstrated powerfully to Stephen and Francine in those early days of their marriage. These friends continued faithful in prayer through the ensuing months, and how they all praised

God together when, ten months after the wedding, the first baby was born to Stephen and Francine. The power of Satan had been broken and the Name of Jesus lifted up! It was a witness and a wonder to Stephen's family, who until this time had been diligent in seeking and obeying the witch doctors' opinions. However, that is jumping ahead a little in the story.

Chapter Four

Great Changes

Stephen and Francine were blessed in so much as they were able to start their married life in their own home. They were very happy, and glad to be together at last. There was one thing, however, which was a difficulty within their relationship. Stephen had experienced such a wonderful change in his life after he had come to know Jesus for himself, and invited him into his life. He was experiencing God's power to change him, and knowing the Holy Spirit directing him and speaking into his spirit. Francine was a good church attender, but as yet did not know Jesus in that personal way for herself. Stephen longed for his bride to be one with him in his faith, which had become the centre of his life.

A week after the wedding Stephen went on his own to the church service, while Francine stayed at home. During the time when her husband was at the church, Francine heard the voice of the Lord speaking to her, saying, "Francine, you think you have been a Christian all your life, but you are not saved!"

She recognised that it must be the Lord who was speaking to her, and she was frightened and confused. When Stephen came home, it was to find a troubled young bride. He asked her what the matter was, and when she told him that she had heard the Lord say these things to her, he was able to explain to her the way to be saved. Stephen then had the greatest joy of all, that of helping his wife give her heart and life to Jesus. Now they were truly one in heart, mind and body. Their marriage could be built on the best foundation of all, a united faith in Jesus.

Later that day it had been arranged that some of their Christian friends would come around and have fellowship with them. Among the group was one of Stephen's sisters. The angels in heaven must have had an amazing party that night because she, too, became a Christian that evening. What a wonderful day it had been!

Francine went to her parents' home to tell her family that she had been saved and now was a real Christian. Although they were regular church attenders, they ridiculed her new faith and commented, "Now you are as mad as your husband!" Their scorn only helped to make her faith grow stronger, and this young couple began to work on how to live out their faith together, not minding the persecution and opposition they were receiving from both their families. In fact, the opposition drew them even closer together, and helped them to depend on each other for support and strength.

Stephen and Francine began to develop a habit of

going out and about together, which is not the normal custom in Rwanda. They went together as man and wife, visiting friends and relatives, to the extent that Stephen's family now thought he had been bewitched by his wife. It was a totally revolutionary practice. Why ever would he want to accompany his wife when she went out? It was unheard of! It was normal for husbands and wives to have a certain degree of conflict between them, and the usual way to resolve this was to spend much of the time doing things independently.

The way in which Stephen and Francine were living their lives became an example to the community around them of a Christian way of living. Other young couples took notice and followed their example, and it helped them to forge strong marriage relationships, too.

During this time, Stephen wanted to express his new faith by taking some responsibility within the church he had been attending at Maranyundo, so he asked if he could become a catechist. A catechist has teaching duties within the church life, but is not an ordained minister. It is similar to a lay reader's position within the Church of England, and was a sign of his commitment to his new faith, that he wanted to study the Bible and teach it to others. He had now left his former life of drinking, smoking and womanising completely behind. The change in her son's behaviour was so remarkable that it caused his mother to question her own way of life, and soon she, too, became a Christian, leaving behind forever her worship of the spirits and attendance upon the witch doctors. The local witch doctor and his entourage were far from happy about her conversion, and constantly hassled her, but she remained firm in her decision to follow Christ. As she reminded them, all their predictions concerning the marriage of Stephen and Francine had been completely false. She told them that they were liars and had deceived her, but now she was a Christian, and had found the truth. She asked Stephen to take her along to the church for baptism as she wanted to make public her conversion. That, of course, was another great joy for him!

His mother was the eldest child in her extended family, and, as such, was the one to whom the other relatives came, to consult when they needed help from the witch doctor, and she was the one responsible for offering the sacrifices demanded. Now she told her family of another way. She would pray with them and for them, but never again would she sacrifice to the spirits.

When the witch doctors visited, they traditionally were given both money and meat. Often a cow would be demanded, even a cow in calf, ready to give birth was once asked for, and given. The witch doctors' power was such that whatever they demanded was supplied, lest they use their power to curse the family. Now that Stephen's mother had renounced the animist beliefs and trusted in Jesus as her Saviour, she determined to give money and meat to the labourers in her plantation, treating them fairly and well, rather than to the witch doctors. Witnessing this miracle in her life is something Stephen and others will never forget.

During these years the Tutsi people were hassled

constantly. They continually faced discrimination and segregation, although the killings had stopped. It was a time of relative peace, during which Stephen was able to work in his banana plantation and raise his cows. Before he was a Christian he had owned a large herd of cows, at least one hundred and fifty. Even so, when he was drunk he thought nothing of stealing a cow from someone else if he felt like it! After he became a Christian the Lord spoke to him about this and told him he had to return the cows he had stolen. When he told this to other people their response was, "Don't be mad! Just keep quiet and let things be as they are!" But the voice inside kept on speaking to him.

The Holy Spirit was saying: You have a choice. Either you can repent of stealing and give back a cow, or you can listen to other people, but they are misleading you.

He chose the way of repentance and restitution, and found, too, that God's way is the best way, even though sometimes it can seem very hard. When he made restitution, those from whom he had stolen were also totally amazed. Nobody in Rwandese culture would admit to wrong, let alone try to make things right again!

There was another hard decision to make, too, after the Lord had spoken to him about his visits to the houses of the prostitutes. He needed to repent publicly and confess this past sin, and he vowed before the Lord that he would never do such a thing again. It was not easy, because so many of his former friends were taunting him and trying to draw him back into the life which he had led before he had met Jesus. He had been very successful, an entrepreneur, a popular 'lad about town', and there were those who were not impressed by his change of life.

Stephen did indeed witness great changes. Jesus had begun to fill his heart with love and, with the security of Francine as his wife, for the first time some of the deep, inner wounds from childhood began to heal. This love began to dissipate the hatred he felt towards the BaHutu people, and instead he began to feel a real love for all his fellow human beings, whichever ethnic grouping or race they happened to belong to. This grew to such an extent that he was able to confess the hatred which he had harboured for so many years within his heart, and he began to socialise with people from all ethnic groups in the community. Stephen found he was able to tell his story of how God had changed his attitude of heart. There was real joy now —he was even able to dance with joy! If he said, "I love you" to a person, whoever they were, it was from his heart and spoken in truth. Before becoming a Christian he could not really say he loved anyone but himself, and when he said those words, "I love you", they were falsehood. Something else had changed, too. From being a man who rarely even smiled, and never laughed, he now found himself spontaneously laughing and smiling!

I looked at Stephen as he told me this. His eyes have a permanent twinkle, and his deep chuckle and laughter so often fill the room that he is in. I cannot imagine this man without joy or laughter; they are now so much part of his nature, and have always been during the six or so years I have known him.

The proof of his changed heart was obvious to all around, but it was demonstrated one day in a particular way. A Hutu man who was now his friend was getting married. He lived some distance away, and in order to attend the wedding and show his friendship for his brother, Stephen walked twenty-five kilometres each way, and he even slept in the family home of this man! They were both Christians and Stephen had a genuine love for him. They were truly friends.

Jesus had changed him in his innermost being, in a way that no influence from parents or a wife ever could. He was a changed man, a new man indeed.

Chapter Five

A Promise of Protection

We take up Stephen and Francine's story again in 1990. This was a tense time when the exiled refugees, mostly from Uganda, but also in other countries in the Great Lakes region, began to plan to return home. This move was led by the *Inkotanyi*, The Rwandan Patriotic Front. Many of these men had been in exile since the popular revolution in 1959, following the death of the last Tutsi king. This was the beginning of Hutu oppression and power, when the old feudal system of the Tutsi aristocracy was finally overthrown. These exiles were bitter about their lot, and wanted to fight back for their rights as citizens of Rwanda. Others who joined this army had been born and bred in exile and had never visited their motherland before. In 1989, in Uganda, Yoweri Museveni's National Resistance Army had been formed, to free Uganda from the oppressive rule of Milton Obote. He recruited and trained many Rwandese refugees to fight with him. Obote had been hostile to the Rwandese refugees, making life in exile difficult for them, so most of them were very favourably disposed to fighting the despot. Up until this point the Rwandese government had not allowed them to repatriate and return to their homes. After Museveni had been successful in his campaign, these soldiers began to plan a strategy, and organise themselves as a fighting force, in order to be able to return and live in Rwanda again.

Meanwhile, in Rwanda, the new Hutu government began to spread their propaganda, teaching that all Tutsi people were undesirables, parasites, not needed in a country which was already overpopulated.

The refugees in Uganda might have hoped that the military *coup d'état* by Major General Habyarimana in 1973 would make a difference and change the policies, but in fact, he reinforced them. He ordered seizure of property and lands owned by Tutsis, and started the resettlement programme into the area of Bugesera. He also imposed educational quotas, making it extremely difficult for Tutsi children to progress beyond primary education, and he also passed a law to prohibit mixed marriages, which remained in place until 1976. Then Habyarimana is believed to have instigated several waves of massacres in the years that followed.

In response to all this, in October 1990, the R.P.F. invaded the North East of Rwanda, crossing from Uganda, hoping to restore democracy. The Rwanda national army soon quelled the invasion with the help of troops from France, Germany and Zaire (Now Democratic Republic of Congo). After this attempt, the Rwandese government took the threat of the R.P.F. seriously and enlarged the national army. Arms were provided by various international communities, but especially by the French, to strengthen the Rwandese forces. The R.P.F. were looked upon as rebel insurgents, even though their declared aim was always to restore democracy and not to overthrow the government.

For the Tutsi people in Rwanda, this 1990 attempted invasion, rather than giving them hope was making their lives increasingly difficult. The war opened the door to end the rule of law. There were swift reprisals. They were accused of being accomplices to the plans and plots. They were told, 'Your fellow Tutsis are attacking us, so we will punish you!' The torture began all over again, and Tutsis were called *inyenzi* (cockroaches) and *ibyitso* (spies), bringing another wave of fear and insecurity. In the Bugesera area, the government officials, police and army began to imprison and interrogate people. There was no way to escape because the citizens were required to produce their identity cards wherever they went, declaring their ethnic origins.

Thousands of Tutsi and moderate Hutus were imprisoned and sentenced to death. Those who dared to question the policies of the government were silenced in this way. The death sentences were not in fact carried out but, even so, many innocent people died from the torture, beatings and starvation. Sporadic fighting and unrest broke out through all the country.

The R.P.F. was now led by Major Paul Kagame. Its previous leader, Rwigema, had died in the October 1990 invasion.

Under Kagame's leadership there were continued guerrilla raids. By 1992 his force had grown to about 12,000 soldiers, consisting almost entirely of Rwandese refugees who lived in Uganda.

The French troops, meanwhile, continued to support the government army. The international community was becoming aware of the situation and put pressure on the president, Habyarimana, to make a number of reforms, including resettlement of refugees. These were drawn up at the Arusha conference. Although he agreed to do this, in fact he did not implement his promises and had no real intention to do so, but wanted to appease the international community. Even so, by nominally agreeing to the conditions laid down at that conference, he made enemies from the most extreme members of the Hutu community. No refugees were ever given permission to return. Habyarimana constantly argued that Rwanda was a very small country and there was no room to repatriate the (now) hundreds of thousands of refugees who wanted to return from far and wide. These Rwandese felt totally excluded from their own land, and became bitter about it and willing to fight for their rights.

In 1991 the political meetings were intensifying, especially those held by the party of President Habyarimana. There were many threats against the Tutsi people. Even professors at the national university at Butare were publishing anti-Tutsi treatises. The two main radio stations were government controlled and supported the campaign to dehumanise the Tutsis.

A list of 'Hutu commandments' was drawn up, which underlined all the measures that had been put into place and the growing hatred which had been festering through the recent years. The list had been devised by the extremists and dictated how a Hutu should regard his Tutsi neighbour. It forbade Hutus from engaging in ordinary personal, social and business dealings with Tutsis, and it imposed severe disabilities on them in many areas of life, including education. It even forbade 'taking pity' on Tutsis, and it was designed to promote hatred. These 'commandments' were widely circulated and were often found hanging in places of honour, in both homes and public places.

People who had previously lived happily alongside their Tutsi neighbours gradually absorbed the propaganda issued from statements like these, as well as from radio broadcasts and newspaper cartoons. Ethnic hatred began to grow, and the ordinary Hutu peasants began to believe that the 'Tutsi problem' was the cause of all the troubles they had ever known.

Even the Tutsi people themselves began to believe the propaganda to the extent that they believed themselves to be worth nothing and undeserving of anything good.

They tried to live quiet lives and not stir up trouble. The few who did manage to get into good jobs, or to universities, were living in a state of perpetual fear. The majority of the Tutsi people worked as peasants on the land or as servants. Almost all job opportunities were denied to them, however well educated they were.

Rwandese journalists who reported on the massacres

which took place from time to time were silenced by dismissal or even prison or death. The government was determined to stop the truth from reaching the international community. France, trying to protect her interests in a francophone country, proved willing to support with money, arms and military personnel, and expertise.

By 1992 Bugesera had become an experimental district, to test and see if a genocide policy would work, and many people were killed at this time. Those who were not killed tried to seek safety and protection in schools and churches. These places did at this time offer a limited degree of refuge. Later, in 1994, when the people again ran to these traditional places of refuge, or were advised to gather there by local officials, it was to be caught in a trap. They were drawn there in order to be massacred. This experiment in genocide was successful inasmuch as the international community did not react. The government realised they could get away with their plans to exterminate the Tutsi people.

The Tutsi people residing in Bugesera were living in a state of tension and fear, not knowing what might happen to them from day to day. This included Stephen, Francine and their family. Fear was once again a daily companion to them.

One day, Stephen was at home praying, and he saw a vision, in which he was preaching and teaching his listeners that they must not hate each other just because they belonged to differing political parties or ethnic groupings. In the vision, as he preached, many people's hearts were moved and they repented, confessing their hate. Stephen believed that God was speaking to him, so he endeavoured to obey the vision by preaching tolerance, not hate. When the local authority officials, who almost entirely belonged to the Hutu Power party, heard of his work, their anger against him increased. He became a marked man, high on the list of undesirables to be eliminated.

Such intimidation made him feel very fearful for his life, and he found his hope evaporating. He knew that he was on the 'death list' simply because he was obedient to the vision the Lord had given him, and was preaching tolerance and love, and also because he regularly held a prayer group in his home, encouraging Christians to pray for peace. Any small group of people meeting together, especially in a home, was very suspect. They were suspected of being in league with the rebel Rwanda army, operating from the Ugandan border.

Stephen knew it would only be a matter of time until the day came when the military police would arrive to arrest him, and take him to the place of interrogation, Gako military prison. One morning, very early, when he was still in his house, he heard a noise outside. He looked out and saw that his home was surrounded by a mob of people, local government officials and the civil and military police. The mob was angry, shouting and threatening the family.

They demanded entrance, accusing him of harbouring rebels in his home. "Bring out your weapons!" they shouted. "We know you have them in there."

"We don't have any weapons," replied Stephen, as calmly as he could.

Then the mob broke into his house, searching everywhere and turning everything upside down. They were intent on destroying everything in their reach, venting their hate and anger on the furniture and household goods. Seeing the whole community rallied against him made Stephen shake with fear and trauma, as he stood trying to protect Francine and their two small children.

Stephen stood transfixed. Seconds seem to pass like hours. He felt as if a film was rewinding in his head. He remembered his early childhood, all the fear and hopelessness, and the ever circling thought, 'The Hutus, they hate us!'

The military forced Stephen to go with them for interrogation. He had been arrested on the charge of supporting the rebel R.P.F. army, was accused of hiding soldiers, keeping their property safe for them, and of recruiting others to join their ranks. Many of the Tutsi men in the area had these kinds of trumped-up charges levelled against them. His family feared, with good reason, that they would never see him again as they saw him pushed into a vehicle and driven away. His mother's house was on the next plot of land, and she, too, thought she had said goodbye to her son for ever.

As a preacher who was actively teaching tolerance and reconciliation, and who was gathering a small group of like-minded men around him to preach this message, he had become hated by the extremists among the Hutu.

They accused him of misleading the people and fighting against the government's policies. These were very serious charges and things looked black for Stephen.

While he was being interrogated and tortured, a soldier passed by the open door of the room and he recognised Stephen. Some of the land where Stephen grazed his herd of cattle was owned by the military, and this soldier had seen him there. He was aware that Stephen was a good man. Something moved within him to use such authority as he had. Even as the interrogators were planning how to kill Stephen, this man was planning a way to rescue him. He was a man of influence and managed to secure Stephen's release after twenty-four hours of detention. It was a miracle orchestrated by the Lord, for it had been intended by the officials that he should be killed while in custody.

Stephen returned home to find an extremely traumatised wife and children. The mob had been very large and intimidating. Francine and the family had been convinced that Stephen would not come through the ordeal alive, so when he returned to them safe and sound, how they praised and thanked God for the miracle of his release! It was like Peter being released from prison, an amazing deliverance!

While he was in detention for those twenty-four hours, the Lord drew near to Stephen in a special way. He saw a spiritual picture in his mind, a revelation that there were two idols in the land of Rwanda. One was ethnic differences, and the other the political party. Both were against the Lord and an offence to him. He was told to warn people against the power of these idols. It was no easy thing to be re-commisioned to go back and preach the same message for which he had been arrested and tortured.

The Lord also spoke to him with a personal message of comfort and reassurance: Stephen, I will secure and protect your life. This was a promise which Stephen needed to reflect on and to hide in his heart, to help him to be strong in the days which lay ahead. He had faced and come through torture and imprisonment and, although he did not yet know it, far worse was to come. He would need to remember and hold on to the promise the Lord had given to him.

Chapter Six

The Growing Threat

Following this traumatic event, Stephen was experiencing inner turmoil, even though he had been released from detention and had heard the Lord promise to protect his life. All around him was hostility and hatred. Daily he was being mistreated by his neighbours and Hutu acquaintances, and he felt the injustice of this so deeply that it became a seedbed of hatred growing afresh in his spirit. The twenty-four hours spent in detention when he was tortured had caused the old emotional wounds of childhood to reopen yet again.

Every day, as he went about his daily business, he was aware that there were questions floating around his mind: 'Why is this happening to me? I have done no wrong! I have never been involved in politics; why should I be accused like this?'

Even with the unceasing questions in his mind, Stephen was hearing another voice speak to him, too. It was the quiet whisper of the Holy Spirit who kept repeating: I will be with you, I will protect you.

It was like being on a see-saw, up and down continuously as he listened to first one voice and then the other. It was also emotionally exhausting for him. The turmoil in his mind was almost more than he could cope with.

Stephen endeavoured to obey the Lord's commission and to continue with his work and teaching as a catechist. The good news of his release spread through the bush telegraph very quickly, and the believers started coming back to visit him in his home. The prayer meetings resumed at the house, although there was a great fear at times when they met together. There was great intensity as they prayed for each other's safety, for the church community, and for their country. They prayed for courage to stand firm in their faith through these days of terror.

The question on everyone's lips was: How will we ever overcome these threats? All the community are focusing on destroying us! How can we escape the slaughter?

Stephen, in particular, was the focus of attention simply because he was the church catechist. He was constantly accused of misleading the people with his teaching, and using his authority to preach against government policy. He preached a message of love and unity in the Lord Jesus, and most certainly the government policy was not in alignment with this teaching! He was repeatedly threatened that the killers would come to his house and exterminate all the believers who met there. At times these threats made them all feel very demoralised, but they tried to encourage each other in the Lord. They knew only too well that these were not idle threats, for

Tutsis and moderate Hutus were being killed every day.

It was at this very low point that Stephen received a fresh understanding of the great power of the Lord Jesus. He realised afresh the truth of the Scripture as he read his Bible one morning. *You, dear children, are from God and have overcome them, because the one who is in you is greater than the one who is in the world* (1 John 1:4).

Once again it was the voice of God he was hearing in this verse. As Stephen read it, he knew it was the living word of God speaking to him at his point of need. Hearing it gave him the strength he needed to speak at a church convention meeting which had been arranged. Even though Stephen knew there were to be soldiers, sent as spies, attending the meeting, he was given the courage to be able to testify about his internment and release. His friends were alarmed when they heard him speak. They felt he had spoken against the military, and government officials, and so there would be bitter reprisals immediately after the service. The church friends were sure that he would be re-arrested and killed that same day. Everyone lived in fear of the Hutu officials around them and kept as low a profile as possible. Here was Stephen preaching boldly and saying how God had delivered him from the hands of the enemy!

There were others in the congregation who declared that his preaching was not from the Lord and that he was indeed a rebel. They were afraid to be seen to side with anyone who might preach a message different from the 'party line'.

Although it was a very difficult meeting at which to testify, the overriding memory for Stephen of that convention is that it was the means of several people coming to a living faith, to which they have remained faithful until this day. Looking back, he knows he was faithful to what the Lord was asking him to do, even though many people misunderstood him and others feared for his life and tried to stop him from speaking.

During these days and weeks the Lord constantly reminded Stephen of his promise to protect and preserve his life.

A pattern began to emerge that would infiltrate even the church community in the months that followed, a pattern of distrust. Who could a person trust? In the climate of the day, your friends, neighbours, fellow believers and even your family might betray you. It was terrible to live in such an atmosphere where you had to watch and weigh every word that you spoke, and wonder about the truth of every word spoken to you.

At this point in his story, Stephen looked at me and paused for a while. Then he commented: "This period of my life will stick in my mind forever. I felt so very close to the Lord and talked to him all the time. The devil really tried every argument to silence me, but even though I was in a place of great insecurity, because of the constant threats, I felt such a compulsion to preach and tell others what God had done for me."

By this time in late 1993 and early 1994, international pressure had been mounting, as facts filtered to the outside world of what was really happening in Rwanda.

The president went to Arusha, in Tanzania, for peace talks which were intended to integrate the R.P.F. into the regular Rwandan army. While this was happening, news was being broadcast on a government controlled radio station. The local Hutu Power officials then turned again on Stephen and warned people that, once the united government army came to Bugesera , he would be shown up for the traitor that he really was, and would never preach again.

By now his family were begging him to leave the country, to flee into exile. Stephen had prayed earnestly and felt it was time to flee, but his old mother did not want to leave her homeland and he could not leave her behind. If they left, they would all leave together, a complete family. No threats would deter Stephen. He kept preaching and testifying, but it was becoming increasingly difficult as the government was fanning the fire of hatred so that no one could trust their friends any more. Fear, suspicion and mistrust were continuing to grow everywhere. In their hearts everyone sensed that something terrible was going to happen.

How do you plan for the future? What do you do? Who can you trust? Everyone was living looking over their shoulders, watching their backs. Even though the prayer meetings continued, all sense of confidence and trust as they prayed together was destroyed.

Stephen repeated over and over to me how the trust between brothers, between families, between everyone was broken down. The propaganda sown in the hearts of people for many years suddenly grew into hatred beyond all imagination. He wanted me to try and understand the terrible fear which engulfed them all, knowing that the whole world was against them, for the international world powers seemed to support the president and the policy of genocide. They certainly were doing little to stop it. Rwanda felt betrayed and forgotten by the outside world. The Tutsi people sensed that they were going to be totally exterminated. The fear was paralysing. People began to accept that this was what would happen, and waited for it. It was as if a great blanket of fate was creeping up and covering them all, extinguishing any vestige of hope that may have remained.

To be a Tutsi meant death. There would be nothing but death to come.

Chapter Seven

The Escape

The purpose of this book is not to give a factual account of the history of those days, but to share the thoughts, feelings and experiences of one man caught up in this utter demonic madness. Most of what is described in this book about the genocide comes from testimony from people who lived in the district of Bugesera, south of Kigali. Atrocities were taking place all over the country. There was no hiding place for any Tutsi, anywhere. The massacres were the most horrific in the districts which held the greatest concentration of Tutsi people. Bugesera came into this category.

"The worst day was April 6th 1994," said Stephen to me. My interpreter, Pastor Jean-Paul, nodded in agreement. Both men were silent for a few seconds. This is a date forever imprinted on the minds of the survivors. Then Stephen continued: "Even though there had already been genocide happening in Bugesera since 1992, now all hell broke out. You must know, it was not all sparked off by the plane crash and the president's death, it was planned, it was all planned. It really started in 1992, but now the trigger had been pulled to initiate wholesale slaughter. We knew it was the beginning of the end for us Tutsis. Nothing would stop the carnage once it had begun."

Stephen knew he had to try to get his family to safety. He could not delay any longer. With a great sense of urgency, on 7th April, he at last managed to persuade his elderly mother that she would be strong enough to walk through the bush to Burundi. It was their only hope of survival, and they knew it was a very slim one. If they stayed in their homes then they would be found and slaughtered without any doubt. So they quickly prepared themselves, knowing they would have to travel light, but not knowing how long they would have to be away from their homes. They had to leave the precious cows, hoping maybe it would be all over and they could return in a few days. It was safest to travel by night because the *Interahamwe* were less active in those dark and cold hours, so Stephen collected about thirty-five of the immediate family together, and they set off, carrying very little with them. It is not easy to negotiate the bush by night, but most Rwandese would be at home eating with their family, and not many Hutu would be roaming around the countryside and likely to see them or betray them. April is the rainy season, and Rwanda's 'winter'. It was quite cold, especially for the elderly and the small children. Stephen and Francine by now had three children. They planned how best to travel. Francine carried the youngest, a baby daughter, on her back, and Stephen's sister put their one year-old daughter on her back. The five year-old son, Claude, was big enough and strong enough to be able to walk alongside them.

The family kept as close to each other as they could, hardly daring to speak. Their mouths were dry with fear. They could only wonder what the night would hold. They prayed they would make it to the border in safety. They travelled, holding on to the fact that the Lord loved them, and knew all about their situation. They were a family where prayer mattered, and they had prayed before they left, committing themselves and each other into the hands of God.

It seemed as if they were doing so well, even though they were tired, cold and hungry. Stephen estimated they had only about another thirty minutes to walk before they reached the safety of the border, when suddenly they were surrounded by an ambush of government soldiers and *Interahamwe*, who at once opened fire on the group. Instantly it was mayhem, screams from the injured and dying, anyone who was able fleeing into the bush, no one knowing where anyone else was. Six of those who managed to run into the bush were quickly caught by the *Interahamwe* and frog-marched all the way back into their village, only to be killed there by their tormentors. They hacked them to pieces with machetes and beat them to death. Only five of the group had escaped the slaughter, but at that point in time Stephen did not know what had happened to anyone else or if there were any other survivors. It was total panic and disarray. The new day was dawning; the raid had been timed for then, so that any escapees would be seen and caught by the *Interahamwe* as the daylight increased. Once the soldiers had recaptured the six they believed they had caught everyone who ran away and that all others in the party must now be dead, so they retreated.

Stephen had managed to run and to hide in the bush. What should he do now? As far as he knew, the killers had gone. His silent prayers reassured him and he felt convinced that he should continue alone and still try to get to the Burundi border post. In order to do this, he had to retrace his steps and return to the place of the massacre, to get on the right path again. In great fear and trepidation, in case there was a trap laid for anyone who might have escaped, he made his way back to where they had been ambushed. As he drew near, he looked carefully and listened for any sound that might indicate soldiers were still there. The coast seemed clear. Stephen could hardly bear to even look where his family lay on the ground. He wanted to just get past the place as quickly as he could, but he thought he heard a baby's cry. He listened again and, yes, a baby was crying, so he edged his way over to where the bodies were lying. In horror and shock he searched through them, gently trying to find where the baby was. Then he came upon the body of his sister, and found that his baby daughter was still alive, strapped to her back. It looked as if the baby was uninjured, and he managed to untie the cloth which held her, and lift out his baby. He held his tiny daughter and quietened her. He praised God she was safe and unhurt.

Stephen then decided that, before he left for the

border, he ought to look and see if anyone else was alive, so he continued to move from one bloodstained corpse to another. It was heartbreaking to see them lying there. His eyes were nearly blinded by his tears as he identified one after another. He could do nothing for them, not even bury them. Stephen had to move quickly and quietly, for at any time the killers could return.

It was then that he saw his son, Claude, blood spattered all over him, and he was sure that he was dead. He had been shot in his arm. Stephen went to walk away when he felt that eyes were looking at him. He sensed a voice telling him to go back, so he obeyed the inner voice and walked back to Claude, and he spoke to him saying, "Little man, do you know me?" for he was sure he was dead.

But the boy answered, "Yes, you are my Dada." Claude was still alive! Praise be to God! Now Stephen had to think how he could take his two children the rest of the way. Claude was severely wounded, and the baby very tiny. How could he carry them both? He realised he could manage if he carried the baby on his back in the traditional way that the women did.

Stephen then retraced his steps and took the *kitenge* cloth from his dead sister's back, and with it he tied the baby on his own back, so that he could then carry Claude on his shoulders. He had to leave everyone else unburied, even his old mother, and hurry away towards the Burundi border. Claude kept begging for a drink of water. Stephen had nothing to give him. His son was very weak because he had lost so much blood from his injury. He kept crying so much that, in spite of all the dangers involved, Stephen bent down and scooped up rainwater from a puddle, in order to quench the boy's thirst. Claude drank from his father's cupped hands.

"It was a miracle," commented Stephen, "that he didn't die from drinking that water! Even the doctor in Burundi said that!"

Again, Stephen paused for a few moments, and then said, "It is my testimony that in difficult times God is always with us."

"I had to go slowly. I could not run with the baby on my back and the child in my arms. It was daylight by now, and I tried to keep under cover as much as I could as I made my way through the bush. I was relieved when I could see the border ahead, about three hundred metres away, and the soldiers there. We had almost made it to safety! My heart really lifted; I believed we would get to safety. Then I heard a noise and saw some more *Interahamwe*. It was a cruel blow!

"Had we made it this far, only to be killed now? I could not run because of the children, but saw a large bush nearby and crawled into it, as quietly as I could. By some miracle the children were quiet, not crying with pain or hunger. The *Interahamwe* had indeed seen me with the children, but thought I had run away down a small path, and they went off that way to capture me. I waited a few moments until they were safely out of sight, then as quietly as I could I climbed out of the bush. I walked as fast as I could, carrying the two children, almost at a run, and reached the border."

As soon as Stephen reached the border post, the

Burundi soldiers at the post came to his rescue. They reached out to him and Stephen knew he was safe! Alleluia! He had crossed the border to Burundi!

The relief that swept over Stephen at that moment was enormous. He had reached a place of sanctuary, and the strong arms of the soldiers guarding the border reached out and took Claude from him. The little boy was still alive, but very weak from the loss of blood and also very traumatised. Amazingly, the little girl on his back had come through the terrible ordeal without being harmed. Stephen was almost naked, his few clothes torn to shreds and covered with blood.

He had no money, no possessions at all. Everything had been lost when they were ambushed. He was completely destitute, and, as far as he was aware, only he and the two children had survived the massacre. His mind was tortured by the memories of seeing all his family dying, the screams, the blood, the sheer raw terror of it all. Now he was a refugee, but the Lord had protected his life as he had promised.

The soldiers took Stephen and the children immediately to a nearby clinic for first aid. Claude needed major surgery, so he was transferred to a large hospital further into Burundi. The separation from his father just added to the terror and trauma the little boy was experiencing. Twelve years later, this young man is still suffering from the effects of those terrible days that scarred him mentally and physically.

Stephen and his small daughter were taken to a refugee camp in north east Burundi. Once registered, he found that Francine had also somehow been able to escape from the ambush, and had managed to reach the border and the safety of the refugee camp, with their other daughter on her back! The Lord had saved the five of them! They had nothing else in the world, but they still had each other. They were the only survivors from their group who tried to leave Rwanda that night.

Chapter Eight

Refuge

The refugee camp held many other escapees from their home area, and some of these were people whom they knew. One such person who helped Stephen was a man who was also a catechist from Marayundo church. He had somehow managed to escape wearing three pairs of trousers, and when he saw the near nakedness of his friend, he gave him a pair. That was a kindness which Stephen remembers with gratitude. It really demonstrated the love of God, for God cared about his humiliation at being naked, and people in the camp needed everything they could lay their hands on for bartering, yet this brother was willing to give such a precious commodity to Stephen. Life in the camp was very basic. They were the poorest of the poor, living under a green plastic sheet. The supplies of food and water were very meagre, and they had almost nothing with which to cover themselves. However, they had their lives, and for this they praised God, even though they had no idea what the future might bring, or if they would ever see home again. Everyone was living with memories of terror and having witnessed scenes of unbelievable cruelty administered to their friends and families. Whenever another person was admitted to the camp they heard more stories of the massacres in Rwanda. Many felt there was nothing left to live for. Almost everyone they knew had been slaughtered. What purpose did their lives have?

They had been in the camp for a week when Stephen started to gather some of the Christians together for times of prayer, and he also began to make enquiries about the churches in the neighbourhood. He found that many of the believers who had ended up in the refugee camp were very discouraged and had lost all sense of hope. They expressed this in some of the questions they asked.

"Does God really exist? If so, how could he allow this to happen to us?"

"Does God tolerate this sort of suffering?"

"If God is really there, then he has some people that he favours and some he neglects!"

All these doubts and questions that were being expressed can have a negative effect on others and pull them down spiritually, too. Stephen himself was struggling, not knowing how to help the little 'flock' which he now had around him. He longed for a fresh meeting with the Lord, that would give him something with which he could encourage these people. He began to cry out to the Lord.

"Then God spoke to me again," Stephen told me, his

eyes glowing at the memory. "He reminded me of the scriptures in John chapter 4, and assured me that the streams of living water still flowed from within me. Then I knew without a doubt that the Lord had not left me, he was still with me. How badly I needed to know that." Stephen wanted to emphasise the assurance which the Lord had given him. "It sank deep within my soul, and only after I had taken it in could I receive the rest of the message. The voice of the Lord then kept telling me to encourage the Christians in the camp, to give them hope and bring them together."

Stephen tried to obey what he felt the Lord had asked him to do. He encouraged the Christians in the camp to come and meet together. He suggested they pray together and praise God for their lives. Although so many of their families and friends had died, they had been spared for some purpose. They needed to thank God that he still had plans and purposes for their shattered lives. Only God could rebuild their lives and families. Stephen also was sure the Lord wanted them to move out of the camp and visit the surrounding Burundian churches. They were not to isolate themselves from the world around them. They had to meet people and learn to trust people once more, even though some of them had been betrayed by other Christians.

It was far from easy trying to help these believers. They were so traumatised and distressed by their experiences, and conditions in the camp were almost intolerable. There did not seem much for which to praise the Lord. Stephen had not appointed himself as their pastor, but the Lord had spoken to him so clearly about getting alongside and encouraging them to be strong in their faith, he knew he had to obey. Even Stephen felt a certain sort of shame in being a refugee, but the voice of the Lord kept asking him to leave the campsite and visit the local churches.

In obedience, one Sunday, Stephen encouraged the Christians in the camp to go with him to a local Burundian church. On the way, as they walked down the road, in some fear and trepidation, not knowing how they would be received, he heard the voice of the Lord speaking to him again: You must be strong and bring my comfort and strength to others. I promised to protect your life and the reason I have kept you safe up until this moment is to do my work.

The Holy Spirit continued to give Stephen direction. He was told when they reached the church they planned to visit he was to ask for an audience to address the congregation. Stephen was told by the Holy Spirit that he was to give thanks and praise to God publicly, even though he was living in such terrible conditions as a refugee.

He heard the voice of the Holy Spirit tell him: Today, you will proclaim me before the people.

Stephen said he instantly said to himself: Whatever am I going to proclaim?

At once a reply came into his mind: You do not have much, but tell the people that Jesus is still alive!

These conversations with the Lord had been so clear, and Stephen remembered them almost word for word, in spite of the passing of the years. Walking down that muddy track in Burundi was a defining point in his ministry. Was he going to live without hope, as were so many around him, or was he going to lift up the Lord Jesus even though life was so very difficult? He knew he had a choice, and it was not easy to say yes to the inner voice.

There is a hymn in the Rwandese hymnbook (number 47 in the supplement) which helped Stephen at that moment in time as he walked along the track to the church. He found it was in his head, and he began to sing it as he went along. I was sitting with Stephen and my translator, Jean-Paul, on the balcony of the house where I was staying. The sun was warm, the birds were singing, and we were sipping sodas. The scene was very different from the one Stephen had been describing to me. I went into the house to find my hymn book, so that he could show it to me, but by the time I came out, the two men were singing this hymn together —a hymn which had spoken so deeply to Stephen during the dark days of genocide.

A rough translation of verses 1, 2 and 4 reads like this:

There still remains a short while to the end of the war,
and then it will end.
A short while and the storm will be stilled,
And then I will rest my head on Jesus' bosom,
Jesus who loves me.
In heaven there will be no sea,
heaven is full of peace.

Pain and suffering are temporary, and the night is also short.
I have always cried in this world,
but that was before I saw Jesus.
In time, a new morning will break and remain.

Now pain and suffering has no impact on me,
I'll forget it when I go to Jesus,
Though I'm still suffering now,
In heaven, no pain, no sorrow, no death.
God will wipe away all tears and will remove
All sorrow, pain and suffering.

I could see that singing this hymn again had moved Stephen, as he remembered God speaking to him through it.

"Spiritually, you could say I was running on empty," explained Stephen. "Even so, I knew I had no option, I had to get up and speak at the church, in obedience to the voice of God.

"We reached the church, just poor refugees, but we were welcomed by the brothers and sisters there. They hugged us and invited us to join them in worship.

"I hesitantly asked for permission to testify, and tell the story of what had happened to me, and it was willingly given, but then my heart just seemed so empty, I truly didn't feel I had anything to say.

"At a certain point in the service, I was invited to come forward and address the congregation. I remember telling the people that I could thank the Lord Jesus, even though I had experienced nakedness, hunger, no shoes on my feet, and multiple wounds on my body; even though

I was like that, I still had Jesus. I still found Jesus was with me, even in that condition.

"When I was well favoured and 'full' in Rwanda, with a house, family, cows, milk, good food, many relatives, Jesus was with me. Now, here, totally 'empty', having lost almost all these things, I have found I can still thank the Lord Jesus, even in my emptiness. Oh I can thank Jesus, because he is still with me!"

Somehow Stephen was given the strength to share this with the congregation, and it moved them deeply as the Lord spoke through him. The Burundians looked at the refugees, who were veritable living corpses, and had compassion on them. They began to visit the Rwandese in the camp and make friends with them, inviting them into their homes to visit their families. Although they were very poor people themselves, they were willing to share what they could with their Rwandese brethren. The testimony to them by the refugees was that they knew Jesus was alive and with them, in spite of all the deprivation and hardship they were suffering. Jesus had been with them and remained with them through it all.

During those months spent in the refugee camp, the Rwandese believers, together with the Burundian brethren who visited, experienced an amazing spiritual revival. This happened through the months from April to July of 1994. In the midst of the horrific evil of genocide, the most savage the world has ever known, God was doing a work of revival, blessing these humble servants with such an amazing awareness of his presence.

Stephen looked at me and sighed. He wanted me to understand something— that the spiritual was far more important than the physical.

"It was so wonderful, so very wonderful! It didn't matter that we had nothing in the physical world. Mary, it really did not matter. You have to believe me when I tell you that! God was among us, we were rich spiritually. Those days in Burundi in some ways were terrible, but in others, oh so wonderful."

I looked at Stephen's glowing face, and knew he was speaking the truth.

Chapter Nine

The Killing Season

No one can adequately record what was happening in Rwanda during those three months of genocide. The bubbling cauldron of hate had finally boiled over. The years of planning and propaganda came to their predetermined conclusion, the almost successful extermination of a people group. The aim was to kill every single Tutsi in the land.

The rocket attack on the plane in which President Habyarimana, along with the Burundian President Cyprien Ntaryamira, were travelling, on April 6th 1994, seemed to be a pre-planned signal. They were coming in to land at Kanombe Airport, and the plane was shot down in the presidential palace garden, which was near the airport. It seems ironic that the president died in his own back garden, but that is where the plane landed. It was reported that the rocket launchers which shot the plane down were manned by foreign soldiers, that white soldiers were seen running away from the guns and no Rwandese soldiers had the expertise to launch the missiles. Instantly, the radio condemned the attack and blamed it on the Rwandan Patriotic Front (R.P.F.), though they could not possibly have done it.

It is reported that within twenty minutes of the crash, from which there were no survivors, orchestrated killings of Tutsis began in the capital city. Death lists had been prepared, detailed lists which named every Tutsi family in Kigali, as well as blacklisting some moderate Hutu families who were known to oppose the Hutu Power regime. So began an orgy of violence. Most Rwandese had access to a radio, and the news spread like wildfire. It appeared that the government soldiers and the *Interahamwe*, were expecting the death of the president, in some way and at some time soon, and were just waiting for orders to implement the plan of genocide. The political opponents of the Habyarimana regime were the first victims, mostly being assassinated by the well-armed Presidential Guard. This guard were very much under the influence of the president's wife and a group of very extreme Hutu men whom she encouraged. The prime minister, Agathe Uwilingiyimana , although a Hutu, was against the extreme policies and had worked hard for a united Rwanda. On 7th April, she was murdered in her home, along with ten Belgian peace-keepers who had gone to her home to protect her. By the following day, many, many other innocent people had met their death at the hands of the violent *genocidaires*.

The R.P.F. had by this time begun to march on Kigali, sending a relief force of 4,000 to try to stop the massacres. There was fierce fighting between them and the national army.

As people listened to the radio, they were advised to stay in their homes, and not to panic. It was part of the strategy, to keep the wanted Tutsis as sitting targets for the killers. In other places the mayors of the towns and prefects of the regions were advising the Tutsis to gather in churches and schools, for safety. This again lured the people into traps, where the maximum number of innocent people could be massacred with the least resistance. The blood lust was relentless, as *Interahamwe* moved from village to village, hill to hill, slaughtering with axes, hoes, machetes as well as clubs studded with nails. In the churches and schools, grenades and guns were used by the militia. Everywhere there were road blocks, and these were ambushes set to kill people who were trying to flee the country and reach the safety of refugee camps in Uganda, Burundi, Tanzania and Congo. People were often tortured before being killed. Children were dismembered in front of their parents before the parents were killed. Women were gang raped before they were killed, sometimes in public places where everyone was encouraged to watch and jeer. Babies were ripped out of the stomachs of pregnant women, and the mother then left to bleed to death. The evil was unimaginable. The roads were littered with the dead and dying. Vultures flew overhead, and dogs acquired a taste for human flesh. It was hell on earth. Those who survived were often mutilated from their wounds. Many women and girls were raped repeatedly, sometimes until death mercifully took over, others left infected with HIV/AIDS, and terrible emotional scars.

The world was experiencing the fastest genocide known in the history of man – almost a million people killed in 100 days – yet it did nothing to stop the horror. Even by 25th April, the UN estimated that one hundred thousand people had been killed and approximately two million displaced since the president's plane had been shot down. The rate of killing was terrible. It was just murder, murder and more murder. Machetes and clubs were literally dripping with blood. Someone has worked out that the rate of murder was three hundred and thirty three and a third murders in an hour, or five and a half lives terminated every minute. In fact, in the early weeks the figures must have been higher than that, as the majority of the killings took place in the first month after April 6th.

Within days, a 'killing season' had begun throughout the entire land.

In regions like Bugesera the Hutu population had been prepared. They had been told the day of their liberation had come. All the men were obliged to take part in the 'killings'. It was obligatory work, even for some boys as young as 10 or 12 years. All schools, churches, football games and other communal activities were stopped, so that everyone would be out at 'work' killing the Tutsi population. The men were organised into work gangs, with overseers from the *Interahamwe*. The work had to continue from morning until late afternoon. Machetes were given out free to those in need. It was the most popular weapon, as most men could wield one easily. They were regularly sharpened. In a culture where obedience to the governing authority was given without question, when the men were told by the local mayor and police to kill the Tutsi enemy or they themselves would be killed, they did as they were told.

Some were timid and reluctant, and others in the gang would support them until they became more confident. If it was thought that they were shirking their duties, then they were in danger of being cut to death too. As time went on, most of the men in the gangs became immune to the horror of it all. Some, however, seemed to revel in cruelty. They conducted their killings with a brutal and fiendish delight, boasting in the evening hours of what they had done and how they had done it. There were some for whom each killing became an adrenaline rush, and the excitement drove them on into excess. They were willing to kill anyone who crossed their path for any reason, even if they were Hutus who had upset them. Some devised more and more horrendous ways of killing. Truly, they must have been possessed by demons.

The rich Tutsis, and those who were not liked because they had offended people, were often captured and tortured, and then murdered publicly in the village, where even the women and children would watch and cheer. The way they were 'cut' and slowly killed was unbelievably cruel.

There were many Tutsi who had run into the papyrus swamps of Bugesera, hoping to hide amongst the tall reeds and thick mud. Many buried themselves up to their necks in mud, but they were ruthlessly hunted down and cut to death.

The women did not generally take part in the hunting and killing. There were some who insisted on taking part, but mostly they were content to loot, or enjoy the fruits of the looting which their husbands brought home.

One policy had been to throw the corpses into the rivers, and bloated bodies were washed up on the shores of Lake Victoria in Uganda. There had been propaganda saying that the Tutsis had migrated from Ethiopia generations ago, and were a Nilotic race, so a 'solution' was to send them back to Ethiopia via the river Nile. The Nyaborongo river that wends its way through Bugesera eventually joins Lake Victoria in Uganda, and so the river Nile.

Women and children were not spared this terrible slaughter, but even when some escaped it was to face a life without family and with such traumatic memories as to make normal living almost impossible.

Nobody was able to trust anyone any more. Sometimes people had betrayed members of their own families, or, even more appalling, actually killed them, when there were mixed marriages between Hutu and Tutsi. Who can imagine such horror?

Yet, as always, in the midst of such evil, stories emerge of immense courage and self-sacrifice. There were some people who did all they could, at the risk of their own lives, to protect and hide their Tutsi friends and neighbours, but sadly many others did not have the courage or the will to do this.

As always, even if people did not partake directly in the killings, there were those willing to take advantage of the situation and went around looting goods and stealing land. Houses were burned, cattle stolen and eaten, the land devastated. Indeed, so much blood was spilt on the ground that it became infertile for a few years.

The killings made people greedy and arguments broke out, particularly over sharing land and banana plantations. At the end of the 'working' day, the *Interahamwe* and the militia took their pick of the loot, leaving the rest to be divided between the gangs of men. It was called the 'killing season' as the Hutus reaped a rich harvest of their neighbours' goods and cattle.

The comparatively few Tutsi people who did manage to escape, either into a neighbouring country, or through hiding for months in terrible conditions, were so traumatised that they had lost all hope of a future. Even twelve years later (at the time of writing this), trauma lies just under the surface in many lives, and they are barely able to lead a normal life because of the terror they suffered during those one hundred days.

So, it is even more amazing that when Stephen and Francine were in Burundi they had an experience of the Lord's presence which was so overwhelming and renewing that they can look back on 1994 as a time of blessing, even though they were living in, and returned to, what can only be described as a living hell on earth.

How do you begin your life again in such circumstances? When Stephen reached his home, which he had built so well for himself and his family, he found it had been completely razed to the ground, and his cattle were nowhere to be seen. Everything he owned had completely disappeared or been destroyed while he was in exile. He walked through the district, and as he walked he found that relative after relative had been murdered in the genocide. Some of his relatives had sought refuge in the Catholic church at the central market town of Nyamata, and others in the smaller church at Ntarama, and had been killed in the massacres which took place in those places. Eighty-six of the wider family of one hundred people had died. The few widows and orphans remaining were now his responsibility.

Several times over the past six years I have visited the genocide sites at Nyamata and Ntarama. Both places have left me feeling shocked and struggling not to vomit. At the large church at Nyamata, twenty thousand souls lost their lives and the remains are buried there. The walls are still bloodstained from where the *Interahamwe* and their cronies grabbed small babies and threw them against the walls to crush their tiny skulls. The roof is littered with bullet holes, the church desecrated. In these days the church meets to worship in a classroom of the school, and the old church building serves as a testimony and a memorial to the dead, bearing a banner with the slogan, 'Never again!'

The smaller church at Ntarama, up in the region of the three hills, is also a poignant memorial. Last time I visited, in 2006, the smell of death still lingered. Strewn around the church between the benches are personal items such as a shoe, an identity card, a Bible, a cooking pot, and shreds of clothing, and bones of people who perished there. Much has been done in recent years to retrieve the remains of the people who died, and they have been re-buried in mass graves in the garden outside, yet it is still a place of devastation, a witness to the demonic evil which exploded within its walls.

When Stephen told me about his relatives dying in these places, it was my turn to become silent and stop the interview for a while. My tears flowed freely. How terrible it must have been for him to come back to Rwanda and find such devastation and to try and grieve in such a place.

Some of those returning found it almost impossible to cope with what they found, experiencing a great sense of guilt that they had somehow managed to escape. Some had so little hope for the future they just wished they had died along with everyone else. Hopelessness, disbelief and distrust hung across the country like heavy black blankets, smothering the life that remained. Where emotions were not completely stifled, they sometimes emerged as hate and revenge directed at the Hutu people who had done this to their families and who still sought their extermination.

The government was trying to stop the threat of revenge killings, and so began to commit thousands of Hutus who had been involved in the genocide to prison. What to do with the prisoners was a problem in itself. At first, they were made to clear the many corpses that were still unburied. Then some were put to work to build new prisons, as there were far too few for the growing number who were being arrested. The overcrowding in the prisons was intense. Prisons built to house hundreds were now accommodating thousands. In some jails the conditions were so poor that there was not room enough for everyone to sit, let alone lie down. Some who stood day and night developed gangrene of the feet and eventually needed leg amputations. Even so, whether because these men felt relatively secure in the prison, or for some other reason, the men were orderly and did not attempt to break out. Their lives were also pretty intolerable, and they had no hope for their future. Many had killed because the authorities had instructed them to do so. They had committed atrocities, but were also pawns in the game, and many of the real instigators of the genocide had fled to Europe or to camps in the Congo.

After Stephen returned to Bugesera, he became aware that the Lord was speaking to him about the prisons. He kept hearing the words of Jesus, "When I was in prison you did not visit me."

He knew that God wanted him to visit and to preach in the prisons, but everything within his being resisted the call. The call became so insistent that in the end Stephen had to take time out and pray, because the struggles within were tearing him apart.

There were two main issues bothering him, the first being that these were the people who had hunted and killed his family. He felt he had nothing good to say to them. The second issue was that hatred had once again infiltrated his own heart and he knew he hated the Hutu people.

He struggled with the Lord, but eventually felt the conviction that he should go and share the gospel of God's love with the prisoners; but he could not do that without first removing the hatred in his own heart.

As he listened to the Lord, the Holy Spirit spoke to him again: Genocide took place in Rwanda because the people did not know or recognise Jesus as the Prince of Peace. Your message cannot impact people until you remove that inner hatred.

As God dealt with Stephen, the tears began to flow. They flowed and flowed, releasing, dealing with the hatred within his heart, cleansing and healing.

Stephen reached for his Bible and turned to Romans 12:17–21 and said, "These were the words that broke my spirit of hatred and changed my direction. I felt God's heart of compassion and forgiveness for these people."

I opened my Bible and read the passage:

Do not repay anyone evil for evil. Be careful to do what is right in the eyes of everybody. If it is possible, as far as it depends on you, live at peace with everyone. Do not take revenge, my friends, but leave room for God's wrath, for it is written: "It is mine to avenge; I will repay," says the Lord. On the contrary:

> *"If your enemy is hungry, feed him;*
> *If he is thirsty, give him something to drink.*
> *In doing this, you will heap burning coals on his head."*
> *Do not be overcome by evil, but overcome evil with good.*

These are very powerful scriptures, and reading them in the context of what Stephen was being asked to do moved me very deeply. However, God's word is for all people in all places at all times, not just for when it might be convenient. Stephen took God's word very seriously and confessed his sin of hatred and revenge, and made a choice that he would walk in forgiveness and love towards all people.

After he had come to this place of submission, the Lord gave him a vision of Jesus on the cross, crying out, "Father, forgive them."

This vision sustained him and gave him the determination and strength he needed to make the first visit to Relima prison.

Chapter Ten

The Prisoners

The battle may have been won in the heavenly places, but it was still a very difficult and tense journey to make to Relima prison.

Relima prison is a grim, brick-built penitentiary, on a hill overlooking lake Kidogo. There is no perimeter fence or barbed wire, to keep prisoners in, or watchtower, with a guard to prevent escapes. The men interned there accept their lot, that this is where they will live until the government decrees otherwise. Two mud tracks lead there; it is a long walk from Mbyo or Nyamata. On visiting days you can see women who may have walked seven to ten hours, with heavy baskets of food on their heads, bringing supplies to their husbands. Visiting days occur twice a week, but many prisoners see their family far less frequently than that. When they do come, after hours of walking, it is to a noisy place, where they are able only to shout a few words of greeting. There is no privacy to talk or restore relationships. The food is hastily given to the relative and then the visitor starts the long walk back home.

From the prison you can see the papyrus marshes of the Nyaborongo river, a grim reminder of the death place of so many of the Tutsi population. Around the prison is an arid area of bush like that to be found in so much of the Bugesera region.

The prison is overpopulated, mostly by Hutu men who killed, raped and looted through the hundred days of genocide. Built to house around 2,500 men, the prison has had to expand to house 7,500. There are blocks in which around 500 men are housed; the triple iron bunk beds have just a blanket and maybe some cardboard for a mattress. About 500 or so men are housed outside under the green tarpaulins, such as are given to refugees, because there is no further space inside.

The prison smells of sweat, rubbish and cooking. It is always noisy, with many groups of men singing, as is the tradition in Rwanda.

The old hierarchy and camaraderie of the killing gangs still exists within the prison, which has made it very hard for inmates to confess their deeds, as there is much intimidation exercised within these groups. The militia and *Interahamwe* are still afraid of the truth being told, so a conspiracy of silence binds them together.

Conditions are very grim within these prison walls, although the government and the Red Cross do send supplies. The government provides corn meal, cassava flour, beans and firewood, and also pays for two hours of electricity each day.

The Red Cross help with oil, medicines, bedding, cleaning supplies and the regulation pink uniforms, which look curiously like pyjamas to the Western eye.

The men may have meagre supplies, but they are regularly provided, which is more than many of their victims have, living in abject poverty, scraping around each day to try to find enough food to eat. This is particularly true of the orphaned children who have no relatives left to support them.

The wake-up call is at 5.30 am, but there are some groups of prisoners who have a practising faith and rise half an hour earlier, in order that they can have time to pray. By 6.00 am the men are making trips down to the lake, with their yellow plastic cans, to collect water for the day. An enormous amount of water is required for washing, cooking and drinking for so many inmates. One meal a day is provided, and the meal is served block by block at any time between 9.00 am and 3.00 pm. It takes so long to prepare food for so many, that they are served all through the day. When visitors bring extra food, it is very welcome!

There are opportunities for the prisoners to work, but it is optional and unpaid. There is work around the prison, keeping it a little less filthy than it would otherwise be, kitchen work, (which has its advantages, as a man can get extra rations that way) and a 173 acre prison farm. Men are also sent out to work on building sites, and it is not at all unusual as you travel through Rwanda to see hordes of pink-clad men on rickety wooden scaffolding, helping to rebuild the towns and villages.

Within the prison there are workshops for mechanics, metalworkers, clock and watch makers and hairdressers.

In the afternoons, chaplains from many denominations are allowed to visit, and they also take services on Sundays. Many prisoners come from Christian backgrounds, and were caught up in the genocide because, sadly, they were sometimes encouraged by their church leaders, and certainly the killings were often condoned. They are glad to have the comfort of services, and it brings something of their former life back into their experience.

The prisoners feel very isolated from the outside world. Many of them have no visitors, and they are all always very wary of outsiders who want to make contact with them. They live in constant fear of reprisals for their crimes. Rwandese culture traditionally embraces revenge as a right when an individual has been attacked.

Repentance, in its biblical meaning, includes facing up honestly to the past and turning from it. Repentance is far more than merely feeling sorry or guilty. It means turning from our sin (and sin is everything that is not in accordance with God's will). It includes turning from the ways of evil, death and false worship and turning instead to Jesus Christ, looking to him for forgiveness and life. He overcame death and won the greatest victory for us, making forgiveness possible, paying the price so that we may be forgiven.

I found it helpful to reflect on this when thinking about the reported attitudes of the majority of the prison population.

Some of the prisoners express sorrow for their actions during the genocide, but very few express real remorse or repentance. The sorrow is often because of the present situation in which they find themselves, rather than sorrow for the families of the people who they killed.

Most of the prisoners are reported to sleep well, untroubled by nightmares or ghosts of their past. Suicide amongst their number is non-existent, although deaths sometimes occur from inmates fighting, or from epidemics of cholera. Malaria also takes its toll, especially as the men are living in such poor conditions.

This describes just something of what life in Relima prison, where the Lord was sending Stephen, was like.

The day came when he plucked up enough courage to make his first visit. He had been given the official permission he required to be able to work there as a chaplain. It was not an easy journey for him, walking over the mud track, to preach to those who had devastated his family clan and denuded him of almost all he had ever owned. It must have gone through his mind: What sort of reception will I receive? Stephen was a well known man in the region, and those who had sought his life were not pleased that he had survived.

When he arrived, many of the inmates were far from happy to learn that this man had come to preach to them. They were suspicious, thinking he had ulterior motives and his purpose was to spy on them and to elicit confessions that would incriminate them or, worse still, that he might be planning to take his revenge and murder them. They could not begin to conceive that he might have pure motives and actually just want to talk to them, and bring the Christian message.

Whenever possible, Stephen tried to visit the prison each week. As he approached the prison, walking along the path, he would be seen and recognised by the inmates who were looking through the windows. The prisoners had devised their own password, which went from room to room and cell to cell: 'The rains have come.' They knew this meant Stephen had come to talk, and they warned each other in this way: 'So be careful that you don't tell him anything! Don't incriminate yourself or others!'

The visits seemed to be fruitless exercises, as everyone was so suspicious of him, and antagonistic. However, he continued to go and preach, week after week, because he felt the Lord had spoken to him so clearly, but it was very discouraging, and he felt more and more like giving up.

Stephen had a problem at home with family opposition, too. The few remaining relatives were uncomprehending and angry when they heard he was visiting Relima prison, rebuking him with questions: 'How can you go to preach to those killers? Are you going to praise and thank them for what they did?'

'Are you bewitched? You are going to those already condemned and beyond redemption!'

Stephen explained to me how he felt torn apart. He was not welcome in the prison, and outside no one was happy with him either. It was a 'no win' situation. It seemed to be an impasse, especially as the weeks stretched into months and even years.

The breakthrough came in 1996. On his weekly visits to Relima prison he noticed the atmosphere was changing and gradually some of the men were starting to respond to the preaching.

Some men began to open up to Stephen as he shared the love of God with them, and they confessed their crimes and truly repented, turning to the Lord for forgiveness. God's grace was at last melting hearts and removing the fear and suspicion, and all the weeks of obedience and perseverance were finally bringing results.

"One day, I will never forget; it is forever burned into my memory," said Stephen. "On that day, we were in the meeting and a man got up in front of everyone and confessed that he had committed crimes against me personally, and my family."

It was a prisoner we will call 'C' who stood up and told everyone how he had been responsible for murder. "I killed your relatives, your family members and many Tutsis," he confessed. "I hated the Tutsis, and, even more, I did not just hate and kill, I was killing Stephen as well. I organised searches for him, and when I could not find him, I destroyed his house completely and all that belonged to him, as a way of convincing myself that I had killed him. In my mind, Stephen, you were dead, I had killed you, too. Even when you came here and I saw you, my mind still kept telling me that I had killed you."

He broke down as he went on to say how the burden of his guilt was destroying him. He told everyone how the very first cup of milk he had ever drunk had been given to him by Stephen's mother, and how his brother had even been given a cow by this family, yet he had turned on them with hate and murder. The guilt he had been feeling in the last few weeks had made it impossible for him to sleep, and he had now come to the place of repentance.

Stephen told me in his quiet and unassuming way, how he was able to run towards C and embrace him and assure him not only of God's forgiveness, but also his own. He knew he had forgiven from his heart. It was not just words, and in an inexplicable way he could feel love and compassion for this man.

As Stephen embraced him, he heard the Holy Spirit speak to him again: This is why I am telling you, you have to visit the prisons.

This encouragement from the Lord was such a blessing as Stephen began to see fruit growing from his ministry.

The year 1996 had seen other changes in Stephen's life, too. Until then, he had worked as a catechist within the Anglican church (very much a supportive teaching and preaching role, helping the ordained priest). Through the genocide the episcopal church was depleted of many of its ministers, due to death, exile and, sadly, even imprisonment. New priests were needed, and the opportunity came to Stephen to be ordained. He was ordained as a deacon, without any theological training, but on account of his life and witness and abilities as a catechist. No one had any doubt as to his suitability and calling to the life and work of the priesthood. It was some time later that Archbishop Kolini ordained Stephen as a priest, as he mentions in his Foreword to this book.

After his ordination, Stephen was assigned to three parishes in Bugesera district: Gashora, Nkanga and Mbyo. It was a huge area to take care of. In the course of time the parishes were divided, and Stephen took charge of Mbyo. He had not only the usual parish duties and services to perform, but also parishioners who were constantly struggling with the trauma of their situations. They needed so much love and care. Many of them were bitter and bound in hate. Many were living in abject poverty as they had lost all their belongings and livestock and they were living in broken down homes. These houses did not always belong to them; they had just found shelter wherever they were able, and so had the fear of being rendered homeless if the owner returned. There was fear and distrust between families and former friends. How do you preach a gospel of love and reconciliation in these circumstances?

Within Rwanda, the government was trying to tackle the immense problem of prisoners and how to administer justice. How could you conduct trials for a million or so murderers? How would it solve the problem if the death penalty was passed on so many Rwandese? What could be done?

Just a few of the leading *genocidaires* had been publicly executed, as Rwanda still has the death penalty as a punishment, but everyone understood that was not the answer to the prison problem. To pass the death penalty on thousands and thousands of Hutu because they killed in the genocide would only further the ethnic hate and divisions, and deplete the country of many more citizens. Some other solution needed to be found. The government was very brave – and somewhat controversial in the eyes of the world – when it found a way through the problem.

The president decided to revert back to the system used generations ago in the villages. It was called *gacaca* (pronounced gatchatcha). The literal translation of the word *gacaca* is 'on the grass'. The idea was that the accused should be tried by the local people in the area where they committed the crime, and the local people would be allowed to give witness as to whether there was any evidence that the accused person was guilty. If the accused also was willing to confess, then the sentence could decrease by half. As the system began to be implemented and has proved a reasonably successful way of trying the prisoners, it has led to a free pardon in some cases. The *gacaca* court in itself did not pass sentence, but if no testimony was given against the person, he could be acquitted if he asked for forgiveness. It is a system of local and traditional justice, but would only work if people were willing to give truthful evidence without intimidation. It was planned through this system to process prisoners more quickly; it would help to re-integrate the prisoners back into their own society. The unknown factor would be the reaction of the victims, particularly in a society where revenge has played an important part in local justice.

The key element was to persuade prisoners to confess to their crimes. There were many men who denied any involvement, and some who refused to answer any question put to them at all. In the prisons, the village hierarchy often still existed, so that the leaders and exponents of the genocide were there with those they oversaw in the killings. They put pressure on these men to prevent them from confessing and incriminating them by telling the truth, for the punishment for those involved at the level of planning and supervising genocide was much greater than for those who were the mere 'puppets'.

The local population were sometimes very fearful of giving truthful testimony, as there were still Hutus around who might carry out reprisals against them. However, in Rwanda everyone living on each of the 'thousand hills' is known to his or her neighbours. No-one is anonymous. Even those who had become successful and were doctors, lawyers or other professionals in the capital would still keep their family land on the hills and be known in the rural areas. The local population would certainly have known who was actively involved in killing and looting and who was not.

The government was willing to give some guarantee of protection for prisoners who confessed, especially as they did communal work to rebuild the areas they had devastated; and, when they entered the community fully again, the authorities helped them to find employment.

When the idea of *gacaca* was introduced, there was considerable resistance to it within the prison population. Nobody was sure how it would work nor whether it could ever be successful, but there was no other way forward. If the prisoners were tried by the Western judge and jury system, it is estimated that it would take two hundred years to try the prison population!

Chapter Eleven

Costly Forgiveness

When the Spirit of the Lord began to move in the hearts of people in the prison where Pastor Stephen was ministering, one prisoner after another began to talk about his involvement in the genocide and was willing to make a written confession. The government administrators recognised the value of this work and so encouraged Stephen to continue with the ministry, for it helped move the idea of *gacaca* forward. Because it was the Holy Spirit who was touching lives, and not just the orders given by officials to the prisoner to confess, then it was the truth which was emerging. It took enormous courage for these men to confess publicly. They faced mockery and violence, even death, from their fellow prisoners and also reprisals from their victim's families. Many of these men, however, speak of the immense relief they felt, once they had told the truth of what they had done. They experienced such a release from their guilt and troubled consciences, which, in turn, brought a restoration of peace in their lives.

As the work of these courts progressed, in order to encourage prisoners to confess, President Kagame, in 2003, passed a decree that those who confessed to the *gacaca* could be released and pardoned. This made it easier for some of the prisoners to confess to Stephen in the prison meetings.

One of these men we shall call 'S'. This is his story.

"The radio broadcasts over the months prior to April 1994 had convinced me that hatred and murder were perfectly acceptable. It was desirable, even my duty as a Hutu citizen, to kill these 'cockroaches'. I went with the gangs of killers, a mob of those like-minded. We had all been brainwashed by the propaganda fed to us by the local authority and the radio programmes. We killed many Tutsis, and among those I killed were six of Stephen's family. Then the R.P.F. arrived and were liberating the country. As they made their way south to Bugesera I was afraid that now I would be killed. When I was captured and rounded up along with other Hutu killers, I was trembling, waiting for a bullet to end my life. I was sure my end had arrived, it was my turn now to die. Instead of a bullet, I received medical help and food. I couldn't believe this was what was happening. I didn't deserve it. We had not shown mercy, why should we receive it?

"I was committed to prison and was coming to terms with living there, when this pastor arrived and started to visit and preach. A shock wave shot through me. I thought he had come to hunt me down and kill me. I tried to hide in the back of the crowd whenever he came around.

"He spoke words about God's love, but I was sure if he ever looked me in the face, he could not speak any words of love to me.

"I was wrong! There was a time when our eyes met, and I heard words of forgiveness. I couldn't believe them. I wanted to show my remorse and sorrow for my evil, so I confessed to my crimes."

After nine and a half years in prison and on confession of his crimes, S was released to a government centre for a three month intensive rehabilitation programme. It was the way that ex-offenders were prepared for life on the outside of the prison, and to help them come to terms with the changes which were sweeping across Rwanda.

S could not help looking over his shoulder all the time, watching his back. He was not convinced that the government did not have an ulterior motive and there would be reprisals for what the Hutus had done. He really thought it was a trap.

After his three months were finished, in fear and trembling he set out for home, the village of Mbyo, where Stephen was now the pastor of the Episcopal Church.

Knowing that S had been released and was returning home, Pastor Stephen had gathered the people together. The people nervously gathered in separate groups, Hutus here and Tutsis there. When Stephen saw what the people were doing, he was upset and knew he would have to confront the situation, or there would never be reconciliation between the two groups.

"This is not the way," Stephen spoke out. "There are no

Hutus now, no Tutsis, we are all Rwandese. We should show love to our brothers."

Having said this, Stephen walked straight over to S and hugged him.

"Something broke inside me when Pastor Stephen did that," said S. "This man cannot be lying or tricking me because he could never hug me like that if he didn't mean it."

Around these two men, other people had taken the cue and moved towards each other and were embracing. Reconciliation had begun in Mbyo.

Since that day, S has sought to share and testify to God's grace and forgiveness in his life, whenever possible. Sometimes this is not easy as there are still people around who do not want the truth told, but he prays for courage and strength to continue. He is now Stephen's friend and helps Francine and the family at the times when Stephen has to travel away from his home. The two families often visit each other and always invite each other to any family celebration. The two men love to go out and minister together in the area, sharing the good news of the gospel, and are living proof that reconciliation and forgiveness are possible in Jesus.

In the prison ministry the Lord was continuing to work. One after another came to confess not just the fact that they had been involved in killings, but also that they had killed members of Stephen's family. A man asked for forgiveness for killing Stephen's maternal uncle, and then another did, too, who had killed one of his sisters. Others confessed to killing and eating his cows, and still others to looting his house.

Stephen found that, through the grace of God, he was able to forgive each one personally. It was not just a blanket state of forgiveness that he had reached in his spirit. Each time he was confronted by a person confessing, Stephen had to face the issue and the hurt and pain, then choose to forgive and give to God the right of revenge, remembering the words of Romans 12:17 that the Lord had spoken to him.

It was not easy, but it was a road that Stephen had chosen to take, and for him there was no going back. If he really believed that God wanted to forgive the sins of these Hutu men who had murdered, raped and looted, then he had to forgive each one and show love to each one, too.

This forgiveness and love was costly. It was more than mere words. It was also costly for some of the Hutu to receive, too. C, for instance, faced so much opposition from his family when he accepted the forgiveness and friendship of Stephen. They did not really trust Stephen's motives and thought the friendship would cause trouble and bring retribution upon them.

Stephen was able to show the reality of his forgiveness to C's family in some practical ways. C, too, had lost his house during the genocide, and Stephen started to help with building him another, even though he had very little time to spare because he was very busy with all his ministries. Stephen recalls the one day when he was carrying water to make mud for bricks.

"I had one large, yellow jerry can on my head, and another in my hand, both full of water", he told me. "I was walking to the hole where we make the mud, when there swept over me such a wave of compassion for C and his situation, I felt I just had to do more. I decided there and then to pay a man to do the water carrying for the rest of the building project, so that the house could be finished."

Stephen didn't say so, but from my knowledge of his situation this would have been a considerable financial sacrifice. Everyone was facing hunger and poverty in Rwanda in those post-war years. Bugesera, and Mbyo in particular, is a dry and arid area, and there is very little water. The water supply was destroyed deliberately by the *Interahamwe* and their cronies. People had to walk long distances to collect water from a well.

C himself was astounded at such practical love and help. "How can Stephen do this," he thought. "He is not even a family member, he is someone who should be my permanent enemy."

There was more! C's wife had left him during the time when he was in prison, and he had not managed to make contact with her. While he was still in Relima prison, he shared this problem with Stephen. Many wives of prisoners found their life intolerable, and remarried or moved away to start afresh. They are often regarded as 'semi widows' in Rwanda. When Stephen heard about C's wife, and that his friend still loved her and wanted to be reunited, he went looking for her. Eventually, Pastor Stephen managed to locate the lady and persuaded her to return home and wait for C.

Once the house was built, and his wife restored to him,

C wanted to have a church wedding. Now he had become a true Christian, the tribal wedding was not enough, he wanted a fresh start, committed to his wife before the Lord, and so he asked Pastor Stephen to perform the ceremony. What a joy that was! All Stephen's family were invited, and that in itself was evidence of true reconciliation! Afterwards there was much dancing and celebration in the new house. The community around, and all the family and friends who attended, were astonished and kept asking, "How can this be? Is reconciliation like this really possible?" It was a living testimony to the power of God to change hearts.

Stephen was invited to other celebrations in the houses of these former enemies who were now his friends. One time he and his family were asked to the home of S for such an occasion. Each time such an event occurred, it was a fresh reminder of the miracles which God had worked. It was beyond human understanding that these families could ever reach reconciliation. Many of these ex- *genocidaires* now live in the immediate neighbourhood of Stephen and his family. The wives chat together and help each other, and the children play together and attend school together without fear. Who could have thought such a thing was possible in 1994? Many of these ex-prisoners have joined the church at Mbyo, or joined with the believers in other denominations that worship in the area.

The work which God has been doing in the prisons has been a powerful testimony in the community to the transforming love of God, his forgiveness for all our

sins and the new life he gives to us when we repent and
return to him.

Chapter Twelve

New Beginnings

It was one of those beautiful mornings when the sun shone in a cloudless blue sky, having burnt off the early morning mist which settled in the valley and clung to the hills around Kigali. My translator, Pastor Jean-Paul, and I were going down to Bugesera to spend the day with Pastor Stephen, and to meet one of his friends. For days he had been telling me how much he wanted me to meet his friend.

The road which leaves the city and winds its way down to the Nyarobongo river which forms a natural boundary of the region of Bugesera, is hard packed red earth. It used to be very rutted and made you feel bones in your body which you did not even know existed! It is the only major road out of Kigali that does not have tarmac, which demonstrated the poverty and neglect of the region. But things are changing! The road had been levelled and was being prepared to be made into a new tarmac road. It will open up the region and is expected to bring new life and prosperity. It is planned that a new international airport will be built in the south of Bugesera that will serve the whole country.

Certainly the area chosen is very suitable as it is flatter than the rest of the country. (Rwanda is famed for its many hills and mountains.) I love to drive through the hills, misty and tinged blue-green by the abundance of the eucalyptus trees which grow on them.

This particular morning, as we drove to the river, hedged by sugar cane and papyrus swamps, I noticed a swathe of bright blue. The water hyacinths were in bloom. It was so beautiful! It was hard to believe that the first time I had crossed over that bridge, in 2001, there was an unexploded mine underneath it, a grim reminder of the genocide. To think that the sleepy river that winds through such a beautiful valley had literally flowed red with the blood of Tutsi victims, and borne its cargo of bloated corpses down to Lake Victoria . . . .

Now a new bridge is being built, ready to take the traffic from the new road. Soon, we will forget the old bridge and road, and they will gradually be taken over by the bush.

Then my mind turned to the people who lived in this region 'over the bridge'. The years will not so easily erase the pain and the memories. These things do not just disappear because life moves on. For so many, the trauma they carry, they will carry to the grave, passing on the fear and the hate to the next generation, unless a miracle happens.

It is that miracle which God is bringing about in these

days, through his obedient servants like Pastor Stephen. His willingness to obey the Lord when he was asked by the Holy Spirit to go to visit those in prison, even though it was such a costly decision, has brought such blessing to others.

Our Land Rover made its way up the road to Nyamata. This town had been so devastated by the genocide. Between April 11th and April 14th, it is estimated that fifty thousand out of fifty nine thousand Tutsis were massacred by machete in the town and commune of Nyamata. Gangs of Hutu militia men and *Interahamwe*, augmented by locals, went to 'work' systematically from 9.30 am until 4.00 pm every day. The 'work' was to kill as many Tutsis as possible.

We drove into the town. It was market day, and there was a great hustle and bustle around the stalls. It was so good to see the produce on sale, evidence of stability, prosperity and regeneration of the area. It is still an area with a very limited water supply, but people are resourceful and working very hard to make a living. On the surface all seems well, but one cannot but be touched by the sadness that is evident in the eyes of so many of the people.

Mbyo is about fourteen kilometres further south from Nyamata, so we continued our trip towards Stephen's home and church. Once we had left the town, the road surface deteriorated. The driver did his best to avoid the many potholes. Every time a vehicle came towards us, we slowed down and put the windows up, to stop the red dust from smothering us all. The last part of the journey was definitely slower than the first part! The land levels out too, becoming more arid and stony. Eventually we turned off the main road and headed up the track towards Mbyo school. Both the church and the school have been built since Stephen moved to be the minister there. The school is a project built by Signpost International and, although unfinished, it accommodates 500 primary children. At the moment they can study up to the class of primary five, but it is hoped in due course, to extend this to primary six, so that children can then continue on to senior education. Before the school was built, there was nowhere for children to be educated in the local area. There are children milling around the buildings, some unable to take advantage of the schooling offered as they have no pencils, exercise books or uniforms. These things have to be provided by the parents. The genocide left many children without parents or extended family to support them. Even where there are some distant relatives, they may be financially unable to fulfil their obligations. It has been such a blessing to some of the children when they have been sponsored by Christians from the West, enabling them not only to get an education, but also to have medicines when they are sick and new clothes and shoes if they need them.

Other children may be waiting for the afternoon shift. There are just so many children needing education that they cannot all squeeze into the classrooms, so the teaching is done in shift systems. The teachers are dedicated men and women who earn very little and may not have had much training, but who are willing to help the next generation. Many Rwandese realise that if people had been better educated then perhaps they would have thought issues through and resisted the genocide propaganda. Education is seen as a priority, a way forward for the next generation. Tutsi children are taught alongside Hutu children without discrimination. If asked, they will not tell you their ethnic grouping; now they proudly explain that they are all Rwandese.

Next to the school is the church. It has already been extended in the six years that I have known it, and it is now a very large mud brick building which can seat hundreds on low benches. On the occasions when I have been privileged to attend this church, it has always been packed. There are several choirs whose tuneful, joyful music-making tells its own story of healing by the Lord.

A few yards away from the church is a small, unpretentious house, again made of mud bricks, overlaid with a layer of cement. Stephen is standing at the doorway, waving a welcome to us! Some of his smaller children are watching, always curious to see a *mzungu* (white person).

The youngest son had been sick with malaria the previous week, but had now recovered. Malaria is still a problem, causing much sickness and death in the village community. Diarrhoea and waterborne diseases are also major problems. Recently a water tank has been installed by a Christian relief agency, and its presence is transforming the lives of the villagers in Mbyo.

Stephen joins us in the Land Rover because he wants

to show me his family land. We slowly make our way along a very narrow track, rarely used by motor vehicles and only just passable. It had rained the night before, and we ploughed our way through deep puddles that covered the entire width of the track. On the sides of the path there were scattered houses, some in a poor condition, abandoned since the genocide, others tidy and lived in, and some new ones were half built. We slowed up to allow a herd of cattle to pass, the typical Ankole cattle with their very long horns. This area is still prized cattle country. Nyamata actually means 'place of milk', and there has always been plenty of milk, both in the town and also in the surrounding district, due to the abundance of cattle and the predominance of Tutsi herdsmen.

Finally, our driver pulls up under a tree, to shade the car, as by now it is very hot. We get out and all I can see around me is bush.

"This is my land," Stephen tells me. "I cultivate vegetables, but further away than you can see from here. This is where my house stood." He pointed to a place a few yards away. I looked, but could see no evidence of any residence at all.

Stephen looked at me searching the landscape and smiled. "See those trees, look at the shape," he said. I looked and could make out that they were growing in a rectangle. I recognised the trees as being the same as were used to form a stockade around the village houses. Most village houses have a neat stockade fence around them, and a certain euphorbia shrub is always used for this. I had never seen the bushes as trees before! Yes, now I could see where a house had once stood.

"Over there," continues Stephen, pointing to the other side of the area, "see, there are the trees which were the stockade bushes around my mother's house."

Both houses had been utterly demolished, and you could only just make out where they had been.

"One day," he continued, "I will rebuild my house." He laughed, his eyes twinkling, "In time for me to retire!"

As Stephen talked to me about his house and its destruction, there was not even a hint of bitterness in his voice.

"I used to own so many cows, more than one hundred cows. Now I have almost none!"

We talked about the cows for a few moments. Like most cattle farmers, he had a great affection for his animals, calling them by name, loving them as part of his household. It had grieved him deeply to know they had been allowed to roam the hills and be killed and eaten by anyone who fancied them. He was sad that the cows had suffered both in the lack of care, and then in being hacked to death.

"One day, I will build the herd again, but for now, I am content."

I could tell that he meant what he said.

We went back to the car and made our way back to Mbyo village. Stephen invited us into his house for some chai — hot, sweet, milky tea, served from a Thermos flask. It is surprisingly refreshing even in the heat of the day. We continued to chat about the family as we drank tea.

Stephen and Francine's own family has grown to seven children, four beautiful children having been born to them since the genocide. Stephen is now the head of his family clan. He directly supports six orphans who live with his own family and eight others who live nearby, and also fourteen widows. There are others, too, widowed in the genocide, or orphaned, who now look to Stephen for support. His family responsibilities are very great, and he tries to do all he can to provide for each one. His eldest son, Claude, has never fully recovered from the traumatic effects of his experiences as the family were ambushed when trying to escape into exile. He has difficulties in learning and is still, aged seventeen, trying to complete his primary education. For the children in the family who have completed primary school, fees have to be found as secondary education is not free.

Francine has a niece whom they tried to help, and for three years they put aside the money and did all they could to persuade her to return to school and complete her education. She refused, her comment being, "What's the point; for me life has ceased!"

Other children in the family come and ask for support and if, as at times happens, Stephen and Francine are unable to provide, they comment, "Why can't you give it to me?" When they are told that there just isn't any more money, then these children remember their father who would have provided, and what happened to their parents during the genocide, and retreat into trauma.

When the widows and orphans in the wider family have no shelter, they seek out the head of the clan and say, "Help me or I die." It is not possible to help them all. If a pastor tells them to reconcile, they answer, "How can I? Those men who did this to me are safe and sound with a roof over their heads, even if it is prison. I miss my husband and can never have him again!"

Stephen is not alone in having these great family responsibilities. Almost every family was devastated and decimated, and many poor households are trying to manage as best they can to feed, clothe, shelter and educate their dependent relatives.

It can also be very difficult for some of the wives of the Hutu men who are still in prison. They may have no means of support for themselves and their children, and also have to try to find food to take to the prison for their husbands.

Then, of course, there is the ongoing problem of the women who have been infected with HIV/AIDS through rape during the war. Living with the aftermath of rape is terrible enough, but for those who were gang raped, or repeatedly raped, often with the intent of infecting them with the AIDS virus, the problems are manifold.

Treatment with anti-retroviral drugs is expensive and not readily available, added to which anyone taking these drugs needs extra food, as the appetite is enormously increased, and in a place like Mbyo, food is often scarce.

One official in the Nyamata region had publicly declared at the start of the genocide that, "A woman on her back has no ethnic group." It gave licence to the Hutu men to rape anyone they wished. Many of the

Tutsi young girls were very tall and slender and had been admired as such by the Hutu men. They were then searched for and used as and when the men felt like it. Those who survived such terrible abuse are emotionally scarred, whether they were infected with HIV/AIDS or not. Some of them feel guilty at being alive, and for the reason they were spared. Some wish they had died, for they feel their fate is worse than death. Some became pregnant through rape and now are left with small children, the harvest of those terrible days. They all need comfort and spiritual help.

These are problems which beset the family and the local community. The church tries to help and support where possible. What it lacks in resources it tries to make up with love. The pastoral work which Stephen has to do is very heavy, yet he still manages to keep to his commitment to go and preach in the prison, and also to spread the message of reconciliation whenever and wherever possible.

We finished our chai, and we all clambered back into the Land Rover, to travel on the road back to Nyamata. A kilometre or so outside the town is the Episcopal Church of Marayundo. There we stopped to meet the friend of Stephen, who was willing to share his story with me. He was a little late in arriving because his grandchild was sick in the hospital, and he had needed to go and buy food for her.

We sat on the porch of the Pastor's house and waited. The church was very near the house, a large building which had come through the genocide almost unscathed.

Stephen recalled standing there on his wedding day and having his photograph taken.

"We no longer have any photographs of our wedding," he told me, shaking his head a little sadly. "They were all lost when our house was destroyed in 1994." We walked over to the door, and Stephen posed for a photo to be taken. Marayundo Church has played such a significant part in his story and spiritual journey.

Then Stephen saw his friend, coming up the hill towards us as fast as he could in spite of the midday sun. They ran towards each other and greeted each other warmly with a hug! There was no doubt that these men were great friends. Their warmth was genuine, certainly not put on for our benefit! I was introduced to 'F'. He looked at me with some apprehension, then looked away, and I knew that his decision to talk with me was a very costly one for him.

We found some chairs and sat in the shade of a large avocado tree outside Marayundo church. It afforded us the privacy we needed, as I did not want us to be overheard. I wanted F to feel at ease. We all prayed together before he began to talk.

He told me just a little of his story. He had been born in the town of Kibuye, in Western Rwanda in 1951 into a Hutu family. Kibuye is a beautiful place on the shores of Lake Kivu, with views over the lake to the Democratic Republic of the Congo. He had been able to go to school, attending the local primary school and completing the first four grades. Then he had to leave and go out to earn a living. In 1975, by now a married man, he relocated with his wife and children to Bugesera and settled in the village of Mbyo. He became the father of six children.

When they moved to Mbyo there was no trouble between the ethnic groups, and F's family knew Stephen's family; they were friends and lived in harmony. He was a member of the local Seventh Day Adventist Church.

Then everything began to change as the local government officials started to alter their attitudes towards the Tutsi population, and forced their doctrines and ideologies on the Hutu residents.

We were reminded of how, after the shooting down of the president's plane on April 6th 1994, the extermination plan went into action the next day and the Hutu population were forced to participate in the killings.

"People killed for different reasons," F explained to me, "but my reason was that the local authority figures had threatened to kill all my family if I didn't join the killing gangs. I felt that I had no choice.

"I only killed one person, and that was at the road block on the Burundi road. It was to stop Tutsi people from fleeing into safety and exile. It was the night Stephen's family fled. I was the one who killed his sister. I was forced to kill her."

F did not want to give any more details of that night, and I did not want to press him. It was obviously hard for him to confess his crime to this *mzungi*, to put into a book. I thanked him for allowing me to tell his story.

F continued to tell me that, after the war had ended, he was taken to prison for his part in genocide and his murder, and he remained in Relima jail for eight long years. He was very fearful when Stephen began to visit the prison, but gradually, over the months, he was able to trust that Stephen had good motives and intentions. It helped him to come to the point where he knew he needed to repent of his sin and make a full and open confession.

Eventually he was able to confess his crime and tell the truth to the judicial authorities, and was given a temporary pardon and release. It was then that he went looking for Pastor Stephen, to ask his forgiveness for what he had done. Stephen's unreserved forgiveness has helped him to become a free man, and to re-integrate into the Mbyo community.

His wife had remained at Mbyo while he was in prison, and had stayed friends with Stephen's family. They helped care for her when they could. She had been faithful to him and visited each visiting day, taking food with her to feed him. She had somehow been able to manage financially through those lonely, difficult years.

"Stephen and I are now able to enjoy each other's company, and even work together. We have a prison association called Umuvumu, (the sycamore tree). There are 264 members in this area alone. It is a fellowship, and we seek to share our testimonies of forgiveness, and to help each other walk with the Lord," F told me. "My church was implicated at times in the genocide, but individuals are coming to repentance. Stephen and I are forming a team of two and going around churches and schools – giving our testimonies and teaching about confession and forgiveness – and demonstrate the fact that unity is possible.

"Once I confessed, my burden of fear was removed," said F. "We, the killers, lived in fear, too. Only God can remove that, through forgiveness."

Our interview finished. The two friends stood together for a photograph, then I was touched as they asked me to join them too. I felt honoured to be trusted with F's story.

We parted, F back to his sick grandchild, and Stephen to walk the fourteen kilometres back to Mbyo, as he has no transport, and Jean-Paul and I to return to Kigali.

Chapter Thirteen

How Could it Have Happened?

What a day it had been! Our Land Rover bumped down the road to Nyamata, and we passed the Catholic Church where over twenty thousand people perished. Every time I see these genocide sites I begin to wonder again, 'What makes a person able to take part in genocide?' We have already seen (in Chapter 9) something of the horror of those terrible days. But how could it have happened? To understand more, we need to think again about the effect that events had on those who were caught up in the nightmare. What made people willing to murder others?

I thought of what F had told me. For him, it was, 'Kill or be killed!' He had only killed once; others went on a killing rampage. I needed to talk to people and read more and try to understand what happened. I needed to re-visit the horror of the 'killing season' and to try to see what forces had been at work.

The human heart is the same the world over. We read

in Jeremiah 17:9, *The heart is deceitful above all things and beyond cure. Who can understand it?* That was a fundamental truth that explained a great deal of the wickedness.

I needed to try more to understand what had happened, not just to judge and at once condemn those who had chosen, or been coerced into, such a path of wickedness.

We returned to Kigali at the end of a long day. Just being in Bugesera again had brought into sharp focus so many aspects of the genocide. What must it be like for people to live where every day you turn a corner and revive a memory? No wonder it is so hard for the nation of Rwanda to reunite and find true reconciliation. It makes it more amazing when you see a man like Stephen, willing to go beyond what seems humanly possible and reach out with the love of God to his enemies, and teach others to do so also.

One reason things happened the way they did was that it seemed it was extremely difficult for some of the Hutu men to say no to the authorities and not participate in the killings. Broadcasting media had played a part in this. Radio programmes had been preparing the way, indoctrinating the population. Not only were the Hutus being taught that they must exterminate the Tutsis, but also Tutsis themselves were often living in such fear that many of them accepted this was to be their fate. This fearful attitude made it easier for some of the Hutu to kill. Rwanda was steeped in a culture of obedience.

There were two radio stars in the early 1990s who

used humorous songs and drama to call openly for the extermination of the Tutsi people, yet they were so funny and clever that even the Tutsis laughed at them. They were very powerful in spreading the message and preparing for genocide. They operated from two radio stations, and as at that time Rwanda was also a radio culture, they reached a wide audience.

In my effort to understand it all, I reflected again on how the local police, government officials, militia and *Interahamwe* had gathered the Hutu men together in a central place each morning in the villages and towns, where they were armed, mostly with machetes. New machetes had been stockpiled ready for this 'work'. Then, when, as we know, they were sent out to kill in supervised gangs, it had been organised and systematic. Those who struggled to kill had been 'assisted' by their supervisors, who finished off the victims, if they had only been wounded. So there had been 'official' pressure.

We can only imagine the group pressure, too, that had been applied. I was told that those who refused to kill were usually killed by the machete themselves, by their fellow Hutus, as they were considered to be traitors to their own people. Moreover, if a Hutu 'turned a blind eye' and allowed a Tutsi friend or relative to escape, then he was liable to the death sentence himself.

I learnt that kindness and compassion had been forbidden. Men had been urged to forget their doubts and become ruthless. They were told not to think about their 'good neighbours', but to forget the past.

Some of the prisoners described how they had soon

become used to the new 'work' described earlier, no longer seeing people as fellow human beings, but rather as animals they had to kill. Daily life had become unnatural, but was accepted, so that in the end, the sight of corpses no longer distressed the killers. They had become hardened to it all. That hardening of hearts allowed the genocide to continue.

I was told that the more they killed, for some, the more the blood lust increased, and at the end of the day the killers would even threaten each other, if a quarrel arose, boasting they were good at splitting a head in two. It is clear that a gang mentality had taken over. Sometimes the gangs were men who had known each other as children or, as adults, had regularly met in the local bars to drink together. They had helped each other in the fields working as farmers, and now they joined efforts and roamed the villages and marshes to kill. The local home brewed banana beer, *urwagwa*, was usually drunk at the end of the day. Sometimes men were even commanded to 'work' again at night. They were all in fear of the *Interahamwe* and local officials, and would not dare to refuse. So much fear — on the part of the killers as well as those who were being killed.

Reflecting further on how it could all have happened, it seems to be significant that some report they felt as if evil demons had possessed them, and 'someone else' took them over and became the killer, yet they allowed this without resistance. This 'person' took and wielded the machete or other instrument of death. Machetes were the most commonly used weapon, because most of the ordinary population were skilled at using them. They were everyday household objects which they had used since childhood. They had learned to use them by watching their fathers. That was the way children learned their farming skills. In the genocide, boys watched their fathers and then tried to imitate and learnt to do the 'work' of killing. That is why special detention centres had to be opened for under fifteen-year-olds after the genocide. Some boys as young as ten years were learning to kill others. I heard a story of boys using the head of a Tutsi lad as a football. This illustrates the way cruelty had become the norm. The men liked to make their victims suffer as much as possible, physically and psychologically, before they finally killed them.

Some men had been frightened and sickened by what they were forced to do. They were intimidated by the gang leaders, and ridiculed in front of the other men if they faltered in their 'work'. Sometimes the more sensitive of the men needed to get drunk first, before they could face the day's tasks.

But the more times a person killed, the less it seemed to touch their mind, as cruelty took over. They had acquired a taste for killing, so much so that even when they were themselves trying to escape to Congo as the R.P.F. advanced, they still stopped to kill any Tutsis they saw en route. The killings had even continued in the refugee camps. In Congo in particular, but also in Uganda, Tanzania and Burundi, some had slaughtered Tutsis who had fled there for refuge, or who were indigenous to the area. Some of the men would testify that they felt no remorse at all, from the first to the last Tutsi they killed. Their only regret was that they did not finish the job completely.

For some, this 'work' had been easier than working on their farms. Most of the Hutu in the Nyamata area were peasant farmers, scratching away to make some sort of living from the earth. They rarely ate meat, only at great occasions like weddings. During the genocide they ate meat twice a day, as they slaughtered the cattle which had been the pride and joy of the Tutsis. It was easy to become lazy very quickly. Why bother to till and plant your own land when you could just loot from the Tutsi homes? Looting was part of the reward for killing. Iron sheets from roofs, furniture, food, radios, whatever you fancied you could take from the homes of the murdered Tutsis. They wouldn't need it any more. Once the *Interahamwe* and other leaders had taken their pick, the men were allowed to help themselves.

We recall that the men found their wives were delighted with all they brought home. They all went to sleep full, whereas in the past they had often been hungry; and they did not have to worry about the weather, the crops or any of the other concerns which usually went with being a farmer.

Some of these poor Hutu farmers had never been to the shops at Nyamata before, and had certainly never eaten bread, cakes or sweets. Now they were the rich ones! It was what the government had promised, they would be the ruling class. It encouraged them to continue with the 'work', and continue until it was completed.

Even the women quickly adapted themselves to this new way of life. Mostly the women did not use machetes, but they supported their husbands. They knew if they hid Tutsis in their homes, and it was found out, then their husbands would be punished. It seemed as if characters and lifestyles changed overnight, once the killings began.

The majority of people had not realised that they were just 'pawns' in the hands of the government, being used to carry out their evil policies. We recall again that many of those who had planned it all in such detail had already flown out of the country to safer places, leaving others to face the consequences of their actions.

Chapter Fourteen

True Hope

Stephen had become a Christian as an adult. All his childhood he had understood that it was his right to pay back and seek revenge against anyone who offended him. It is the African tradition, the way that grievances are settled. It meant that Stephen needed to completely reverse his thinking in order to deal with his enemies, and he wanted to explain to me the spiritual journey he had undertaken to find the Christian way of dealing with offences.

"It is a great miracle," he told me, "such a great miracle, because of the depth of pain and resentment I held in my heart. For a long time, I just held to the Old Testament teaching, 'eye for eye and tooth for tooth' (Exodus 21:24). It made me think that revenge was scriptural and acceptable. I was happy to believe that, even though I was trying to calm down my own feelings of trauma, hatred and bitterness. I felt I had a God-given right to revenge, so I could hang on to my feelings of hate, it was okay. God understood, I had suffered so much. I had a right to my feelings."

Stephen often pauses when telling his story, sometimes to see if I have correctly understood what he is saying, but often because he is reflecting on the significance of what was happening at that point in his life. It was that sort of pause we came to at this moment.

"It was so great meeting the Lord in such a wonderful way in the refugee camp in Burundi, and to experience revival. I didn't want to lose the closeness to the Lord I had found, so when we came home after the genocide I needed to get alone with God, and allow him to speak to me. It was very important for me to listen and to hear. One such time, I was quiet before him, listening for the Holy Spirit to speak to me, when the words of Jesus came so powerfully, from Matthew 5:38–48. Could you believe that ten verses from the Bible could turn your life around?"

Because they impacted Pastor Stephen so much, I am quoting them in full here.

"You have heard that it was said, 'Eye for eye and tooth for tooth.' But I tell you, Do not resist an evil person. If someone strikes you on the right cheek, turn to him the other also. And if someone wants to sue you and take your tunic, let him have your cloak as well. If someone forces you to go one mile, go with him two miles. Give to the one who asks you, and do not turn away from the one who wants to borrow from you.

"You have heard that it was said, 'Love your neighbour and hate your enemy'. But I tell you: Love your enemies and pray for those who persecute you, that you may be sons of your

Father in heaven. He caused his sun to rise on the evil and the good, and sends rain on the righteous and the unrighteous. If you love those who love you, what reward will you get? Are not even the tax collectors doing that? And if you greet only your brothers, what are you doing more than others? Do not even pagans do that? Be perfect, therefore, as your heavenly Father is perfect."

Stephen continued:

"Also the Lord reminded me of the scripture I told you about before in Romans 12:14–21. As I contemplated these words and what God was saying to me, I began to see spiritual pictures in my mind. I don't know whether they are visions, I call them that. They were pictures of Jesus, as he was in the New Testament. I began to argue with Jesus, 'So Jesus, why are you asking of me more than I can bear? Don't you really know and understand what has happened in my life?'

"Then I argued with myself: how can Jesus really ask me to do this when he knows my sufferings from childhood right up until the present moment?

"I longed to be a true son of God, (Matt 5:45), but the conditions were too hard, I could not make a decision to follow and obey with all my heart. It seemed as if Jesus had forgotten what it was like to be in this world, and I told him so. I accused him of not remembering all the mistreatment that I had taken. It wasn't fair to ask so much of me."

Once again Stephen paused. Once again I waited; I knew his next words would be important.

"Then I remembered how much Jesus had suffered,

too," he said quietly. He continued, "I went on to look at the next verses of Matthew 5 — verses 46–47. If you love those who love you — well, the evil ones do the same, what is the difference between you? As I thought and prayed, I really didn't want to go to visit and preach to the people whom I hated, but I also prayed that in the end I wouldn't fail to receive eternal life. It seemed to me, as I read verse 47, that it was telling me that I should be different from the pagans, the *genocidaires*. I knew what the Bible said was true, but it was such a painful struggle.

"Then I continued to verse 49, and as I read it I thought about the genocide. There were Christians who got involved in the killings and looting, even some ministers and church leaders. I was now crying before the Lord: how can I be different?

"It was a cry from the heart, and the Lord responded in the still small voice of the Holy Spirit: Stephen, you need to get rid of all the bitterness and hatred within your inmost being. Then, and only then, what you long for will happen. You will reap a harvest from the act of forgiving."

Stephen was deeply and profoundly impacted by this word into his heart. It reminded him of another place in Scripture, when the prophet Samuel was sent by God to Jesse, to anoint one of his sons to be the king of Israel. One by one the sons appeared before the prophet, but none of them was God's chosen. God spoke to Samuel and said that men look on the outside, but God looks upon the heart.

Stephen knew he had to listen to the voice of God, to

obey that voice. Again he heard the Lord speak and he explained that what you see in this world, all the evil around you, is due to people thinking and behaving differently to the way God is, his true nature. If they acted in the way God does, were like he is, then the world would be different.

It was a challenge to Stephen to be willing to be different, to act and think differently from those around him. It was the challenge of the Beatitudes (see Matthew chapter 5). Believers are to be salt and light in their society. "You cannot be salt and light if you harbour bitterness and unforgiveness in your heart. If you do that, you are no different from anybody else around you," Stephen explained. "I was having a huge battle in my mind whether I could be different."

These were the thoughts and scriptures which led Stephen to a place where he was willing to lay down his own hatred, and to give up the right of revenge. It had to be done, a private transaction between Stephen and his Lord, before he was able to live it out in the community.

Once he had come to this place of confession and cleansing, he was able to testify to others because he knew a change had happened in his heart. As he shared with other people what God had been doing in his heart over these matters, he found that it was helping them, for almost everyone had the same spiritual problems with hatred and unforgiveness after the horrors of genocide. "It is a spiritual pattern, a principle which I learnt," said Stephen, "that before I could help others, I had to be helped and receive the benefit of the teaching. Before this point, I was so full of bitterness, I had no peace in my life, and I was heavy burdened. I would try so hard, and pray and pray out loud, but I still had no peace. The wounds got covered over, but never healed."

There were many friends who were experiencing the same difficulties in praying and who had no peace. When Stephen began to talk about the spiritual battle he had been through, and the journey he had made that gave him peace again and removed the bitterness, there was a response and others came to the Lord for healing. His testimony seemed to break the deadlock of the bondage which held so many people captive. Looking at Stephen's radiant face as he shared this part of his story, I am sure that alone would be enough to convince others of the truth of the peace he had regained.

Until this time he so hated going back to his former home area. Whenever he saw the place where his house had been, it filled him with anger. Stephen felt he could never again live in that neighbourhood. After this encounter with the Lord, and the healing of the inner hurts and removal of the pain, he began to think of returning and reclaiming the land from the bush. Stephen realised he could work on the land and grow crops for his family and dream of the time when he would rebuild the house. He could now visit the place without anger and hate rising up inside him every time he looked at it.

Previously, when Stephen had to make the trip to the land, before the Lord had dealt with the issues, he always went in the daylight. He was too scared to travel there at night. But now he found he felt quite differently — the land held no demons for him. The Lord had restored his peace to the extent that he was able to look at the demolished buildings without bitterness, no longer troubled that he had once owned a well-built, strong house.

For many of the survivors of the genocide, shelter and security are very big issues. The loss of homes has been devastating. When there is no extended family with whom you can live, and your ancestral land has been taken from you, the three basic needs of mankind, significance, self-worth and security, are threatened. This, in addition to the horrendous trauma already suffered, makes life almost impossible for some of these people. Their only hope is to find the inner healing that Jesus can bring. This is why Pastor Stephen's testimony has been such a lifeline to his people.

Various aid agencies and the government have been working hard to build little housing estates. They are called *umugadugudu*. These small, brick-built houses are close to each other and usually close to the main road. It is helping people to be resettled, living with the security of close neighbours instead of the isolation of small holdings all over the hills. It means that the people have to travel out to farm their land, but they are able to sleep more peacefully at night because they feel more secure. Settlements like these have also been built for special groups of needy people: the widows and the child-headed families, orphaned during the genocide.

Security of housing has helped many, but it does not remove the trauma and hatred.

When the survivors see someone like Pastor Stephen who has a real hope in his heart, it impacts them greatly. They see that there can be hope for them, too. So many Rwandese have lost their hope, and living has been reduced to a mere existence. It becomes a case of just trying to get through each day, doing the ordinary things and trying to block out the memories.

Many of the churches had been desecrated by massacres in 1994, and nobody wanted to use them again for worship. However, Rwanda was a largely Christian country, and people began to gather for worship in other places, like school classrooms, while they constructed new churches. The congregations gradually increased in these places as the population began to find God again.

Stephen began to have the courage to share his story in these churches, at any community gatherings, even at funerals. It did take courage, too, as most of the Tutsis thought he was a traitor to his people, reaching out with love and forgiveness to their enemies. He himself was becoming more and more aware that this was more than a testimony, it was a growing ministry which the Lord was blessing. The message of repentance and forgiveness could impact Rwanda. How else could this ravaged country and devastated people ever hope to recover? Stephen saw a glimmer of hope. He had found hope again in his life by sharing what he had learnt in his spiritual journey. Could he help his country find a new hope?

It was soon after this that he was contacted by the Prison Fellowship of Rwanda, a branch of the International

Prisons Fellowship, and asked if he would co-ordinate a programme of reconciliation in the district of his parish of Gashora.

Chapter fifteen.

Chapter Fifteen

Steps Towards Reconciliation

When the Prison Fellowship of Rwanda had heard about Pastor Stephen and realised that he had experienced a wonderful healing in his own life and was working towards reconciliation, they knew that he was both respected and trusted in his community, and that was essential for the work which they were trying to do.

The ministry in Gashora has two main aims: to preach unity and reconciliation, and to build and provide shelter for those made homeless through the genocide.

The Prison Fellowship International is a global association of one hundred and ten national Prison Fellowship organisations. It is active throughout every region of the world, with a network of more than one hundred thousand volunteers working for the spiritual, moral, social and physical well-being of prisoners, ex-prisoners, their families, and victims of crime. The movement is trans-denominational.

It was able to give exactly the support and encouragement that Stephen needed in his ministry in the prison.

The fellowship has several programmes. These include the following:

COMMUNITIES OF RESTORATION

A number of Prison Fellowship Organisations operate faith-based prison units as an alternative approach to prisoner rehabilitation and prison management. These in-prison communities foster the spiritual and moral regeneration of prisoners by helping them understand their own human dignity as well as that of others around them. From this foundation, prisoners assume responsibility for themselves and seek to contribute to the lives of others. It is based on a model developed in Brazil more than thirty years ago. This faith-based initiative has yielded remarkable recidivism rates of 5%–12%.

HUMANITARIAN ASSISTANCE

In many prisons around the world, extreme overcrowding, poor ventilation, food shortages and substandard sanitation conditions lead to the rapid spread of serious and chronic diseases among prisoners. The limited resources of some developing nations often results in inadequate or non-existent medical care for prisoners. PFI's Global Assistance Programme mobilises teams of volunteer doctors and nurses to conduct short term medical assistance in these prisons. Since 1995, over six hundred medical professionals and support volunteers have brought relief and hope to more than ninety-five thousand prisoners and prison communities through PFI's Global Assistance Programme. PFI has also partnered with the Swiss Army to provide medical equipment and supplies to prisons in developing countries around the world.

SYCAMORE TREE PROJECT

Prison Fellowship International's unique victim/offender mediation has had a dramatic effect on participating prisoners. The Sycamore Tree Project brings victims into prisons to meet with unrelated offenders in an intensive 8-12 week course, in which they discuss the consequences of crime. The results are profound for both victims and prisoners. A recent survey of more than 2,000 prisoner participants showed an improvement in their empathy toward crime victims and their recognition of the harm their individual offences have caused, as well as a decreased sense that crime is worth the cost.

In the Episcopal Church Stephen was greatly respected as a minister, and held three posts within the archdeaconry of Bugesera. He was the minister of Mbyo Parish Church, held office in the Department of evangelism, and was chairman of the Healing Committee.

As chairman of the latter, he works closely with the diocesan counsellor, and together they have held workshops, using the Sycamore Tree model for inner healing. Over three hundred people have attended these and found some relief from their inner pain. Even more people have attended the large conventions and received teaching on healing and reconciliation. It has been a great encouragement to Stephen to see many people find a new peace and hope in their lives.

There have been seminars too, that addressed the needs of couples who have had difficulty in their relationships, especially since the genocide. It has been such a delight to see these couples begin to relate mentally, physically and spiritually once more. The trauma had been so great that even husbands and wives had felt distrustful of each other, and needed time and loving help to rebuild the bridges.

Of course, the majority of the population are still harbouring ethnic hatred, on both sides of the divide. The main work is to try to reconcile these groups, to bring the Tutsi and Hutu people together so that they can live as brothers. Sometimes this work can be very slow and discouraging, but the joy when people do reconcile and live together in peace is a wonderful reward, which makes all the hard work worthwhile. Stephen states that one very special joy is to see people who have sat together in church, on the same bench, who hated each other, come together in true love and forgiveness. It is still a big problem for the churches to try to move forward into reconciliation and unity.

Stephen related to me the story of one man who attended a seminar for healing. This man had been grossly maltreated by his own father. This father had deprived him of any education, so the man felt all his future had been stolen from him. All he felt in his heart for his father was hatred, so much so that he wanted to kill him. At the seminar he came to a place of repentance and cleansing. After he found his forgiveness in Christ, he was able to offer forgiveness to his own father, and found love, instead of hatred in his heart.

There were many others who had bad family relationships which were destroying themselves and those around them. When they were willing to allow Christ to deal with their hearts, they found restoration, to the extent that now a real Christian community has been built. Some of these people then have been willing to come forward and testify to the truth at the *gacaca* courts. It has been a great leap forward for these courts, as the past experience has shown that so few people are willing to speak and give evidence and, if they have done so, then they have been very evasive and economical with the truth. There has to be truth spoken for these courts to work, and for the community who gather at them to recognise and appreciate they are hearing the real truth and that *gacaca* is a valid way forward for a new, integrated Rwanda.

So Stephen was able to organise the Prison Fellowship ministry programme in this way. There are ten parishes within the archdeaconry, and he has been able to form a committee in each one of them, who are willing to oversee and run the programme. Some of the parishes have asked the churches of other denominations to join them, and that has been a great success. It is bringing a harvest of reconciliation to the area.

The vision is to take the programme to every small village in the entire district. This will be quite a task, as transport is not readily available. Only very recently have funds been provided for Pastor Stephen to buy a bicycle. Before this, he walked many, many miles, through extreme weather conditions, unless someone with a motorcycle or car was able to take him. However,

Stephen is undaunted by this. He longs to see a strong church, built on real unity and free from hypocrisy.

Implementation of the programme of reconciliation seminars for the Prisons Fellowship has been helped by African Evangelical Enterprise of Rwanda. They recognised the special needs of Bugesera, as it had been so neglected, people were so exceptionally poor, and the genocide had been so devastating. They have approached the problem from a different angle, but with the same aim, healing through the gospel of Christ and reconciliation of Hutu and Tutsis, to live together in Christian community.

At the present time, Stephen, along with some of his now close friends who were former enemies, are starting a programme of taking the message of reconciliation to the local schools, both primary and secondary. They are trying to teach the children not to get involved in ethnic hatred, but to live together in harmony. They are helping the children to understand that they are primarily all Rwandese, not just Tutsi or Hutu. They need to be part of the new Rwanda where everyone is equal and respects each other. Stephen and his colleagues are sharing their personal stories and the needless horror of the past, and testifying to how they have been able to reconcile through the grace and love of Jesus. It is a constant source of amazement to the audiences that a Tutsi and a Hutu can do this work together.

In the school holidays, longer seminars have been held for the children, in a similar format as for the adults, but geared to their special needs. Stephen remembers the glowing embers of fear and hate that were planted in his heart as a child, and longs to prevent it happening in the lives of the new generation. They may have been born since the genocide, but will have absorbed the attitudes of ethnic distrust around them. If they can learn while they are still young, then there is real hope for the future.

The school work is still in its infancy, held back, again by the lack of transport, but the vision is to visit in due course every school in Bugesera with the programme.

Another area which the prisons fellowship is trying to address is bringing together and creating good relationships between the families of prisoners and the families of victims. Using the Communities of Restoration model, they are attempting to hold seminars where they are able to meet each other and to learn of each other's problems. Again, it is not an easy task, but hearing the testimonies of families who have forgiven their neighbours and now live together in harmony has a powerful effect.

Poverty since the genocide has been a great barrier and hindrance to reconciliation. The programme is therefore trying to help in very practical ways. Small mutual associations have been formed, which are microfinance schemes. These have been found to work very well amongst the widows of the genocide, so now the prisons fellowship and the diocese are trying to form similar self-help groups. The Kigali diocese has helped by giving goats to each group, to help them get started to become self-sufficient.

The groups help each other in very practical ways, such

as building houses, helping with school fees, health bills, agriculture, etc. They have become fellowship groups, too, giving spiritual support to each other and studying the Bible, praying and singing together.

At the end of the session in which Stephen was telling me about this work, his final comments were, "We need prayer support. We need God to help us where we cannot help ourselves. We are deeply committed to relieving poverty because we believe reconciliation and unity will be tangible when people are not so poor."

Chapter Sixteen

"My Beloved People"

I wanted Pastor Stephen to tell me a little of how he approaches a congregation, and what truths he presents to them. That request made him beam with his huge smile. Stephen is a preacher and loves to share the truths from the Bible!

"I try to share three main truths," he said —

1. Jesus' teaching about forgiveness and repentance.
2. The first Adam brought pain and death, but Jesus is the new Adam.
3. Adam caused the world to be at war, without peace.

"When I come to explaining the third point, I do not think that Adam, who sinned, brought genocide. Sin came to one small family via Adam. Look at the biblical story in Genesis 27:1–13. Ethnic differences are not the only sin to cause divisions between people. We see it in small families, like that of Rebekah. There was this great division between the two brothers, even though they were twins. After all that happened between them, God was eventually able to bring reconciliation to the family. In this story I see that the offender can ask forgiveness, but also, the offended can offer forgiveness, too.

"Look at Genesis 32:23 and the following verses."

We both opened our Bibles – my English NIV and Stephen's Kinyarwandan edition. We read the few verses that describe how Jacob met with God, on his way back to his childhood home.

"You see," explained Stephen, "before Jacob reached his old home, he had to go through many struggles within himself, and these struggles originated in the things which he had done to his elder brother. I tell my people, once you are helped by the Holy Spirit, you can repent and repent fully, as Jacob did when he confessed his name, Jacob (I'm cunning). (See v. 29.) In confessing his name, he admitted his sin, that he was a cunning man who had plotted and carried out evil against his brother.

"This is where my hope lies," continued Stephen. "Someone who has gone very far can be changed. God changed the name of someone very cunning to 'Israel'.

"If such a change and reconciliation is possible between families who have offended each other, then it is even possible between ethnic groups, between black and white races, between anyone. *He himself went on ahead and bowed down to the ground seven times as he approached his brother* (Genesis 33:3). This is when Jacob exposed what God had done in his heart. He went ahead of his family, and had to prostrate himself seven times. Seven times symbolises total repentance. Then, he instructed his family to do the same."

Stephen continued with his exposition of this chapter: "You see, Jacob was saying: when I left home I had a bad reputation, but now I go home a different person! When I am teaching, I stress that if a person confesses and repents, it is not enough just to say a few words, it has to be accompanied by practical demonstration. Some Christians only utter the words, and it all ends there. It is not enough. I tell my people that Jacob was strengthened by his meeting with God, and I pray that they will also have a meeting with the Holy Spirit. When full repentance – convicted by the Holy Spirit and not by the police or the courts of law – occurs, then what happened in Genesis 33:4 can happen again."

We read the verse together. *But Esau ran to meet Jacob and embraced him; he threw his arms around his neck and kissed him. And they wept.*

Stephen continued, "What happened here between these two brothers was not human, it was an act of the Holy Spirit! The Spirit enabled Esau to forgive fully, without hypocrisy. The cause of the separation had been very real and very deep. No-one was denying that. Jacob had only just escaped with his life, for his brother was out to kill him, hunting him for his blood. The way he welcomed his brother back was supernatural. The Bible says he went 'running' not 'walking', then 'embracing'. They hugged each other, they kissed each other, and wept. This was for real! This is a picture of brotherhood!

"My teaching is that through the Holy Spirit it is possible to both give and receive forgiveness, even after deep betrayal. No-one else was involved in bringing these two brothers together, it was an act of God.

"Verses 8 and 9 show how real the repentance and forgiveness was. Jacob was saying, in fact: I want to share with you. But Esau was replying: No! What I want is YOU! Forgiveness is not dependent on what you can give, it is total acceptance in love!"

Stephen stopped and looked at me and questioned the translator. He wanted to be sure that I understood his reasoning and thoughts.

"Do you understand?" he asked. "This is why I believe, and am truly convinced, even after genocide, the Rwandese community can come back to being one!"

I nodded, I understood, including the reason why Stephen wanted this book to be called, 'After genocide, there is hope!'

"Reconciliation in Rwanda is possible!" Pastor Stephen emphasised again.

Pastor Jean-Paul and I said, "Amen!" in unison. We believe it, too!

"My prayer is not only for the Rwandese, my beloved people, but also for all of troubled and divided Africa, that they might find this way of reconciliation" was Stephen's final comment to me.